Contents

Folder Centers

Individual Practice

Partner Practice

Math Centers
Take It to Your Seat

What's Great About This Book

Centers are a wonderful way for students to practice important skills, but they can take up a lot of classroom space and require time-consuming preparation. The 15 centers in this book are self-contained and portable. Students may work at a desk or even on the floor using a lapboard for writing. Once you've made the centers, they're ready to use any time.

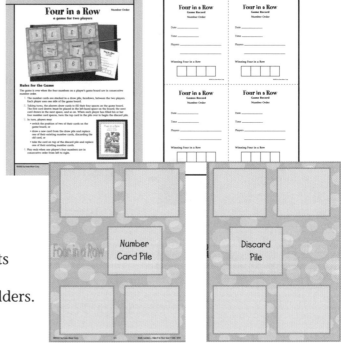

Everything You Need

- Teacher direction page
    How to make the center
    Description of student task

- Full-color materials needed for the center

- Reproducible answer forms

- Activities for different levels of difficulty

    You determine the level appropriate for your students and include the sets of task cards for that level in the folders.

- Answer key

Using the Game Centers for Partner Practice

The centers on pages 111–190 are designed for partner practice. Considering these questions in advance will avoid later confusion:

1. Will students select a center or will you assign the centers?

2. Will there be a specific block of time for centers or will the centers be used throughout the day?

3. Where will you place the centers for easy access by students?

4. What procedure will students use when they need help with the center tasks?

5. Where will students put completed work?

6. How will you track the tasks and centers completed by each student?

Making a Folder Center

Folder centers are easily stored in a box or file crate. Students take a folder to their desks to complete the task.

Materials

- folder with pockets
- envelopes
- marking pens
- glue
- tape

Steps to Follow

1. Laminate and cut out the cover design. Glue it to the front of the folder.
2. Place answer forms, writing paper, and any other supplies in the left-hand pocket.
3. Place each set of task cards in an envelope in the right-hand pocket.

On Sale

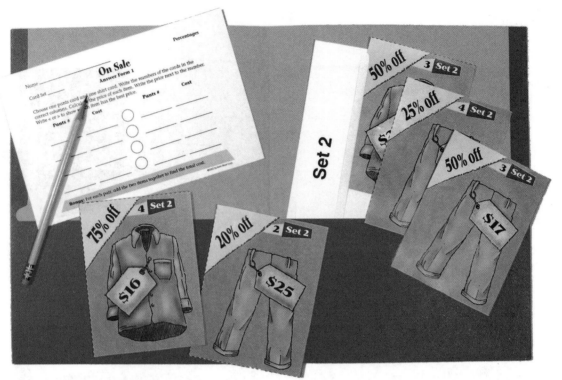

Preparing the Center

1. Prepare a folder following the directions on page 3. Laminate and cut out the cover design on page 7. Attach it to the front of the folder.

2. Laminate and cut out the pants and shirt cards on pages 9–19. Place the pants and shirt cards in each set into an envelope, label the envelopes with the set numbers, and place the envelopes in the right-hand pocket of the folder. (Page 6 provides blank cards. Add numbers of your own and reproduce a supply.)

3. Reproduce a supply of the answer forms on page 5. Place copies in the left-hand pocket of the folder. **Note:** Answer Form 1 gives students an easier bonus job than Answer Form 2.

Using the Center

1. The student chooses one pants card and one shirt card.

2. The student calculates the price of the pants and the price of the shirt using the original price and percentage off tags.

3. The student records the price on the answer form.

4. Then the student writes the appropriate symbol in the blank to tell which item has the lower price.

5. The student repeats the process until all cards in a set have been used.

Name _____

Card Set _____

On Sale
Answer Form 1

Choose one pants card and one shirt card. Write the numbers of the cards in the correct columns. Calculate the price of each item. Write the price next to the number. Write < or > to show which item has the best price.

Pants #	Cost		Shirt #	Cost
_____	_____	◯	_____	_____
_____	_____	◯	_____	_____
_____	_____	◯	_____	_____
_____	_____	◯	_____	_____

Bonus: For each pair, add the two items together to find the total cost.

©2002 by Evan-Moor Corp.

- -

Name _____

Card Set _____

On Sale
Answer Form 2

Choose one pants card and one shirt card. Write the numbers of the cards in the correct columns. Calculate the price of each item. Write the price next to the number. Write < or > to show which item has the best price.

Pants #	Cost		Shirt #	Cost
_____	_____	◯	_____	_____
_____	_____	◯	_____	_____
_____	_____	◯	_____	_____
_____	_____	◯	_____	_____

Bonus: For each pair, add the two items together to find the total cost. Determine what percentage of the total the shirt is.

©2002 by Evan-Moor Corp.

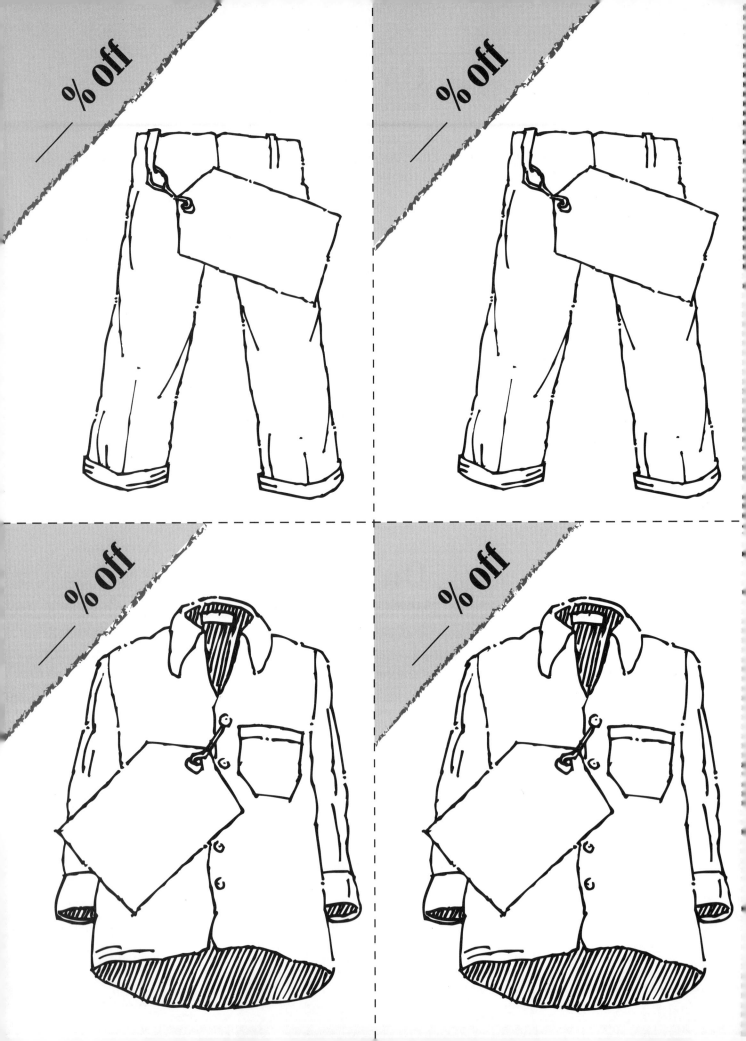

On Sale
Percentages

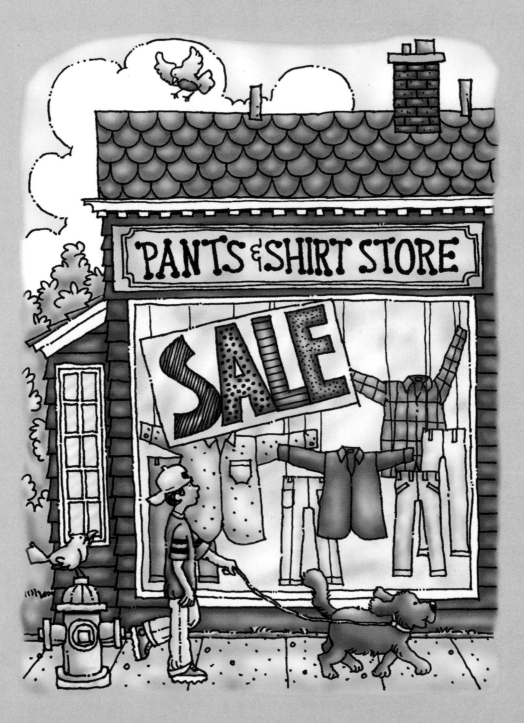

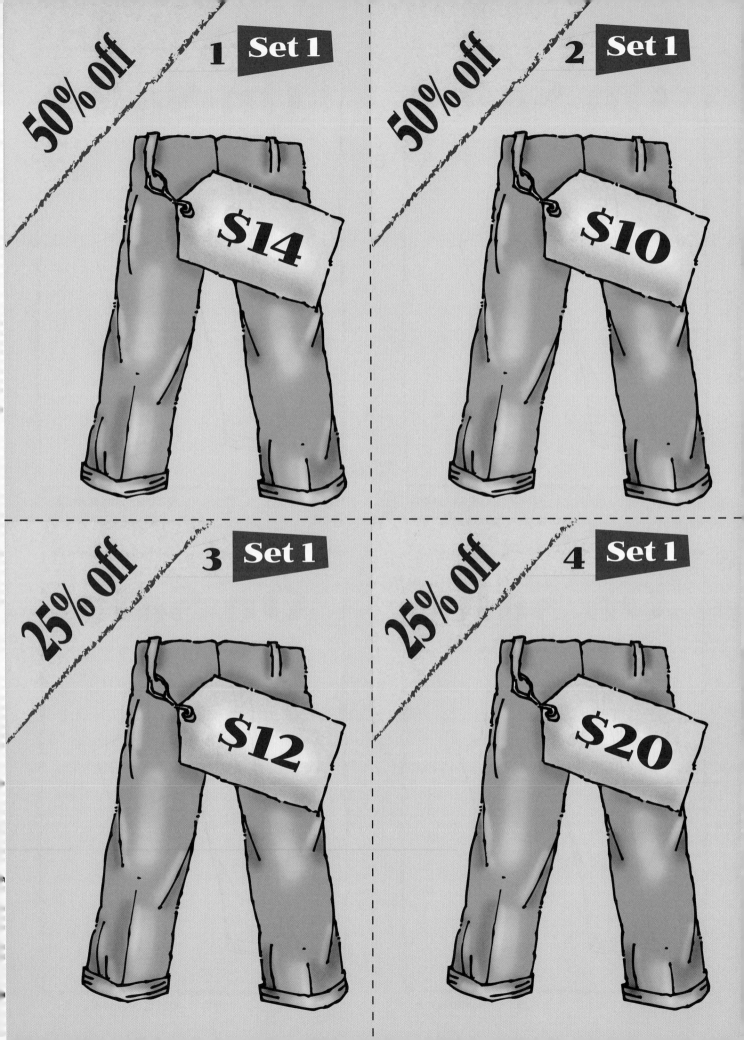

On Sale
Percentages

On Sale
Percentages

On Sale
Percentages

On Sale
Percentages

50% off **1** **Set 1**

$8

25% off **2** **Set 1**

$16

50% off **3** **Set 1**

$18

25% off **4** **Set 1**

$10

On Sale
Percentages

On Sale
Percentages

On Sale
Percentages

On Sale
Percentages

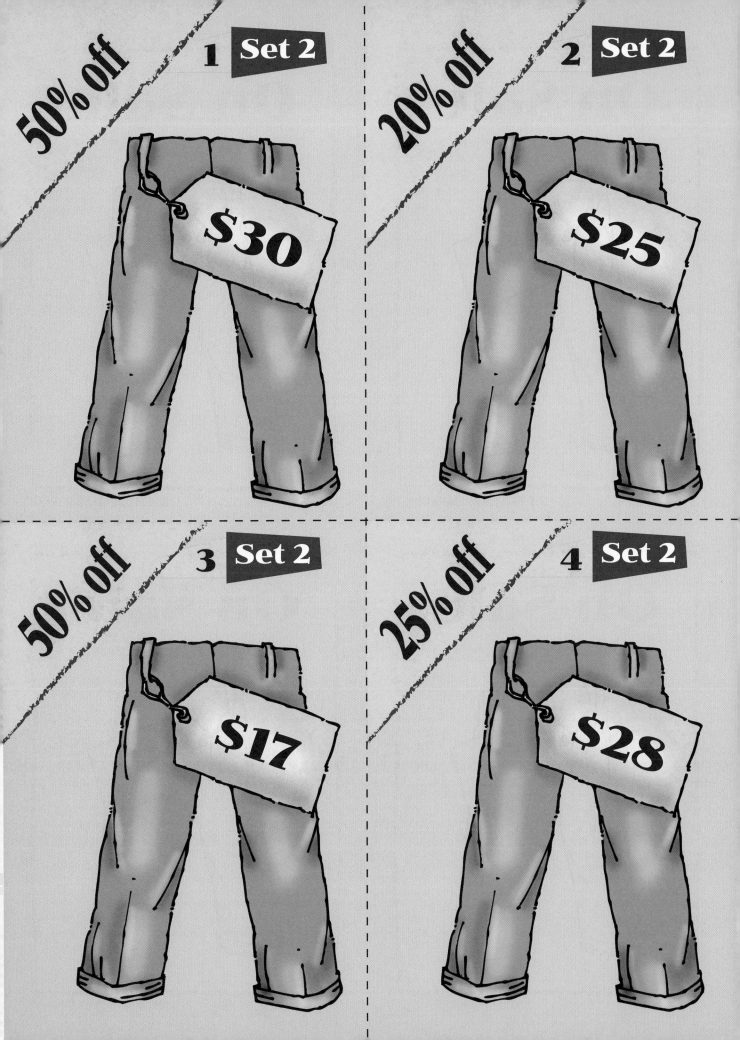

On Sale
Percentages

On Sale
Percentages

On Sale
Percentages

On Sale
Percentages

50% off **1** Set 2

25% off **2** Set 2

50% off **3** Set 2

75% off **4** Set 2

On Sale
Percentages

On Sale
Percentages

On Sale
Percentages

On Sale
Percentages

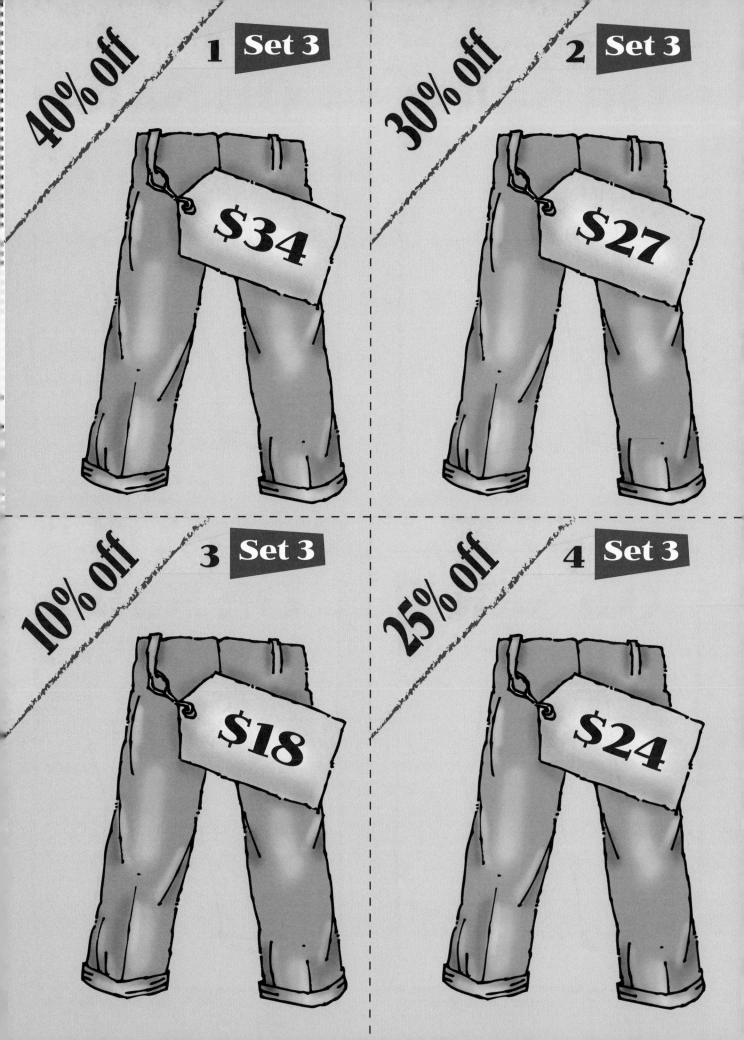

40% off   1 **Set 3** $34

30% off   2 **Set 3** $27

10% off   3 **Set 3** $18

25% off   4 **Set 3** $24

On Sale
Percentages

On Sale
Percentages

On Sale
Percentages

On Sale
Percentages

50% off 1 **Set 3**

$19

20% off 2 **Set 3**

$26

40% off 3 **Set 3**

$21

30% off 4 **Set 3**

$17

On Sale
Percentages

On Sale
Percentages

On Sale
Percentages

On Sale
Percentages

In Balance

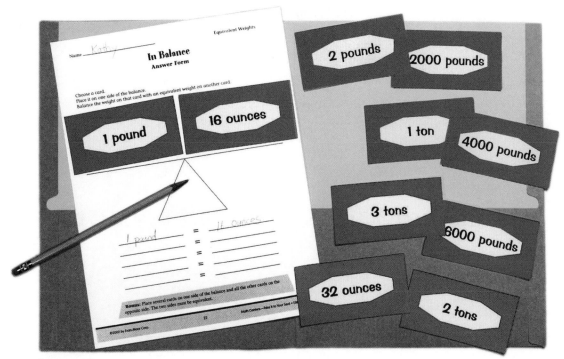

Preparing the Center

1. Prepare a folder following the directions on page 3. Laminate and cut out the cover design on page 23. Attach it to the front of the folder.

2. Laminate and cut out the task cards on pages 25–29. Place each set in a separate envelope, label the envelopes with the set numbers, and place the envelopes in the right-hand pocket of the folder. (The cards progress from easy to hard—red, blue, green, respectively.)

3. Reproduce a supply of the answer form on page 22. Place copies in the left-hand pocket of the folder.

Using the Center

1. The student selects an envelope and spreads the cards out on a flat surface.

2. The student chooses one card and places that card on one side of the balance on the answer form. The student copies the number on one of the lines below.

3. The student looks through the remaining cards to find an equivalent weight to balance the first. When the card is found, it is placed opposite the first card and the number copied.

4. The two cards are put aside and two more cards are "balanced" and copied.

5. Repeat until all cards have been used.

In Balance
Answer Form

Choose a card.
Place it on one side of the balance.
Balance the weight on that card with an equivalent weight on another card.

Place one card here.   Place equivalent card here.

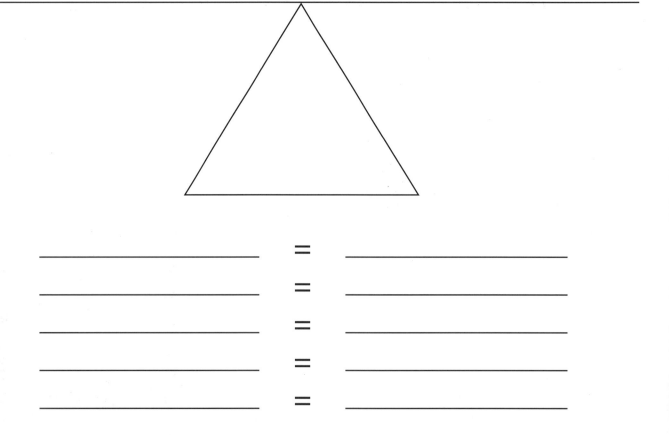

_____ = _____

_____ = _____

_____ = _____

_____ = _____

_____ = _____

Bonus: Place several cards on one side of the balance and all the other cards on the opposite side. The two sides must be equivalent.

In Balance
Equivalent Weights

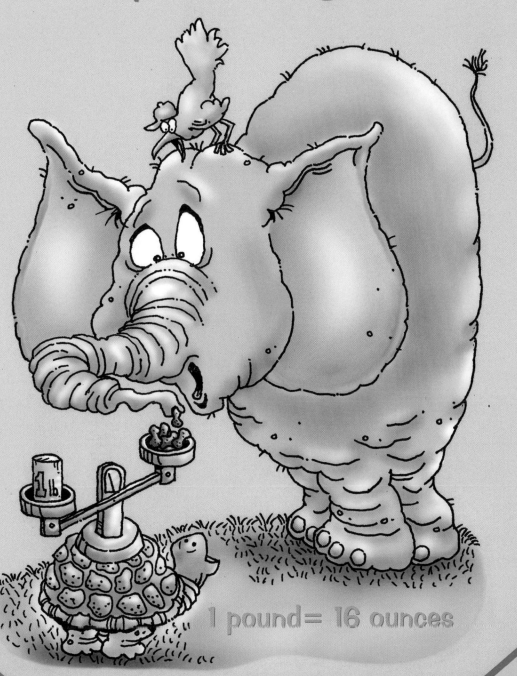

1 pound = 16 ounces

1 pound	16 ounces
2 pounds	32 ounces
1 ton	2000 pounds
2 tons	4000 pounds
3 tons	6000 pounds

In Balance
Equivalent Weights
©2002 by Evan-Moor Corp.

In Balance
Equivalent Weights
©2002 by Evan-Moor Corp.

In Balance
Equivalent Weights
©2002 by Evan-Moor Corp.

In Balance
Equivalent Weights
©2002 by Evan-Moor Corp.

In Balance
Equivalent Weights
©2002 by Evan-Moor Corp.

In Balance
Equivalent Weights
©2002 by Evan-Moor Corp.

In Balance
Equivalent Weights
©2002 by Evan-Moor Corp.

In Balance
Equivalent Weights
©2002 by Evan-Moor Corp.

In Balance
Equivalent Weights
©2002 by Evan-Moor Corp.

In Balance
Equivalent Weights
©2002 by Evan-Moor Corp.

$1\frac{1}{2}$ pounds	24 ounces
100 pounds	1600 ounces
10 pounds	160 ounces
25 pounds	400 ounces
50 pounds	800 ounces

In Balance
Equivalent Weights
©2002 by Evan-Moor Corp.

In Balance
Equivalent Weights
©2002 by Evan-Moor Corp.

In Balance
Equivalent Weights
©2002 by Evan-Moor Corp.

In Balance
Equivalent Weights
©2002 by Evan-Moor Corp.

In Balance
Equivalent Weights
©2002 by Evan-Moor Corp.

In Balance
Equivalent Weights
©2002 by Evan-Moor Corp.

In Balance
Equivalent Weights
©2002 by Evan-Moor Corp.

In Balance
Equivalent Weights
©2002 by Evan-Moor Corp.

In Balance
Equivalent Weights
©2002 by Evan-Moor Corp.

In Balance
Equivalent Weights
©2002 by Evan-Moor Corp.

1 kg	1000 g
1 g	$\dfrac{1}{1000}$ kg
50 g	$\dfrac{1}{20}$ kg
10 g	$\dfrac{1}{100}$ kg
100 g	$\dfrac{1}{10}$ kg

In Balance
Equivalent Weights
©2002 by Evan-Moor Corp.

In Balance
Equivalent Weights
©2002 by Evan-Moor Corp.

In Balance
Equivalent Weights
©2002 by Evan-Moor Corp.

In Balance
Equivalent Weights
©2002 by Evan-Moor Corp.

In Balance
Equivalent Weights
©2002 by Evan-Moor Corp.

In Balance
Equivalent Weights
©2002 by Evan-Moor Corp.

In Balance
Equivalent Weights
©2002 by Evan-Moor Corp.

In Balance
Equivalent Weights
©2002 by Evan-Moor Corp.

In Balance
Equivalent Weights
©2002 by Evan-Moor Corp.

In Balance
Equivalent Weights
©2002 by Evan-Moor Corp.

What's Your Angle?

Preparing the Center

1. Prepare a folder following the directions on page 3. Laminate and cut out the cover design on page 33. Attach it to the front of the folder.

2. Laminate and cut out the task cards on pages 37–41 and the protractors on page 35. Place them in envelopes, label the envelopes, and place them in the right-hand pocket of the folder. **Note:** Protractors may be reproduced as transparencies for easier use.

3. Reproduce a supply of the answer forms on page 32. Place copies in the left-hand pocket of the folder.

   Note: Answer Form 1 asks students to count the angles of the figures that they create. Answer Form 2 asks students to use the protractor to measure the angles. Students using Answer Form 1 will not need protractors.

Using the Center

1. The student chooses a task card and plots and labels the coordinate points.

2. The student connects the points in order to form a closed figure.

3. The student counts or measures each of the angles in the figure.

4. Students who have measured the angles add them and record the total.

Name _____

What's Your Angle?
Answer Form 1

1. Choose a task card.
2. Plot and label the coordinate points.
3. Connect the points to form a closed figure.
4. Count the angles.

Task Card # _____

How many angles? _____

How many sides? _____

What's the name of the shape?

_____

Bonus: Draw two other figures with the same number of sides as the one you have already drawn. Label the figures. Write the coordinates of each corner point.

©2002 by Evan-Moor Corp.

- -

Name _____

What's Your Angle?
Answer Form 2

1. Choose a task card.
2. Plot and label the coordinate points.
3. Connect the points to form a closed figure.
4. Use a protractor to measure each of the angles.
5. Find the sum of the angles.

Task Card # _____

Sum of the angles _____

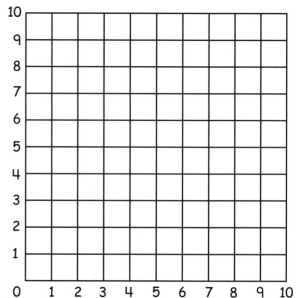

Bonus: Draw two other figures with the same number of sides as the one you have already drawn. Measure the angles. Calculate the sum of the angles. What observation can you make about the sum of the angles for each of the figures?

©2002 by Evan-Moor Corp.

What's Your Angle?

Coordinate Graphing
Measuring Angles

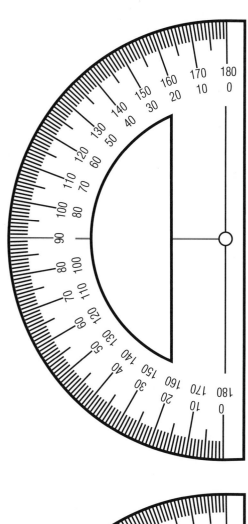

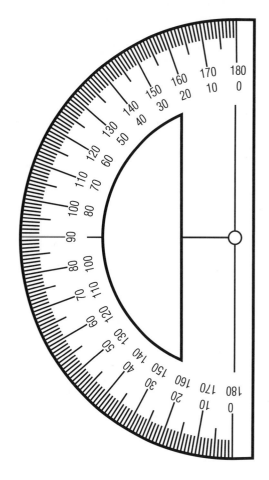

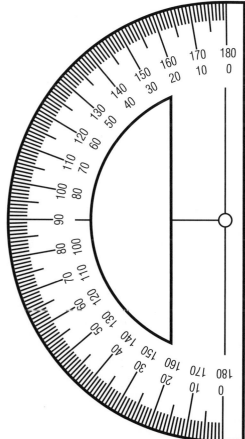

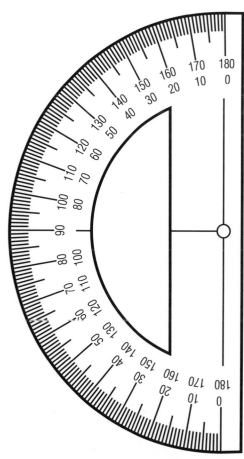

1

A = (3, 1)
B = (8, 1)
C = (8, 7)

2

D = (2, 2)
E = (8, 3)
F = (5, 6)

3

G = (1, 5)
H = (10, 5)
I = (9, 8)
J = (5, 8)

4

K = (5, 6)
L = (2, 6)
M = (2, 3)
N = (5, 3)

5

O = (1, 1)
P = (7, 1)
Q = (7, 8)
R = (1, 6)

6

S = (7, 5)
T = (9, 5)
U = (9, 7)
V = (7, 7)

What's Your Angle?

Coordinate Graphing
Measuring Angles

©2002 by Evan-Moor Corp.

What's Your Angle?

Coordinate Graphing
Measuring Angles

©2002 by Evan-Moor Corp.

What's Your Angle?

Coordinate Graphing
Measuring Angles

©2002 by Evan-Moor Corp.

What's Your Angle?

Coordinate Graphing
Measuring Angles

©2002 by Evan-Moor Corp.

What's Your Angle?

Coordinate Graphing
Measuring Angles

©2002 by Evan-Moor Corp.

What's Your Angle?

Coordinate Graphing
Measuring Angles

©2002 by Evan-Moor Corp.

7

W = (1, 1)
X = (4, 1)
Y = (3, 5)

8

Z = (4, 2)
A = (10, 1)
B = (10, 4)

9

C = (6, 1)
D = (10, 5)
E = (9, 6)
F = (5, 2)

10

G = (7, 4)   J = (1, 8)
H = (7, 8)   K = (1, 4)
I = (4, 10)

11

L = (3, 5)   O = (4, 9)
M = (5, 5)   P = (2, 7)
N = (6, 7)

12

Q = (7, 7)
R = (10, 7)
S = (7, 10)

What's Your Angle?

Coordinate Graphing
Measuring Angles

©2002 by Evan-Moor Corp.

What's Your Angle?

Coordinate Graphing
Measuring Angles

©2002 by Evan-Moor Corp.

What's Your Angle?

Coordinate Graphing
Measuring Angles

©2002 by Evan-Moor Corp.

What's Your Angle?

Coordinate Graphing
Measuring Angles

©2002 by Evan-Moor Corp.

What's Your Angle?

Coordinate Graphing
Measuring Angles

©2002 by Evan-Moor Corp.

What's Your Angle?

Coordinate Graphing
Measuring Angles

©2002 by Evan-Moor Corp.

13

T = (3, 1)   X = (5, 7)
U = (5, 1)   Y = (3, 7)
V = (7, 3)   Z = (1, 5)
W = (7, 5)   A = (1, 3)

14

B = (3, 1)
C = (6, 3)
D = (5, 9)

15

E = (6, 1)
F = (9, 1)
G = (10, 7)
H = (7, 7)

16

I = (8, 1)
J = (10, 9)
K = (7, 9)

17

L = (1, 6)
M = (7, 6)
N = (9, 9)
O = (3, 9)

18

P = (1, 7)
Q = (8, 8)
R = (3, 10)

What's Your Angle?
Coordinate Graphing
Measuring Angles
©2002 by Evan-Moor Corp.

What's Your Angle?
Coordinate Graphing
Measuring Angles
©2002 by Evan-Moor Corp.

What's Your Angle?
Coordinate Graphing
Measuring Angles
©2002 by Evan-Moor Corp.

What's Your Angle?
Coordinate Graphing
Measuring Angles
©2002 by Evan-Moor Corp.

What's Your Angle?
Coordinate Graphing
Measuring Angles
©2002 by Evan-Moor Corp.

What's Your Angle?
Coordinate Graphing
Measuring Angles
©2002 by Evan-Moor Corp.

Tangram Puzzlers

Preparing the Center

1. Prepare a folder following the directions on page 3. Laminate and cut out the cover design on page 45. Attach it to the front of the folder.

2. Laminate and cut out the tangram pieces on page 47. Laminate the task cards on pages 49–55. Place them in an envelope and put the envelope in the right-hand pocket of the folder.

3. Reproduce a supply of the answer form on page 44. Place copies in the left-hand pocket of the folder.

Using the Center

1. The student chooses a task card.

2. The student tries to make the shape on the card using the set of tangram pieces.

3. The student records the number of the task card on the answer form and tells whether a solution using all of the pieces was possible. If the puzzle was solved, the student traces the shape and draws in the lines to show the solution.

Tangram Puzzlers
Answer Form

Choose a task card. Try to solve the puzzle. Record the number of the card. Tell whether it can be solved. If you solved it, draw lines on the figures below to show the solution.

Task Card # _____

Can it be solved using all of the pieces?   Yes   No

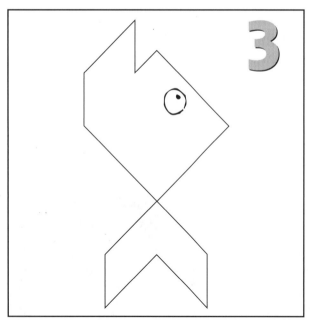

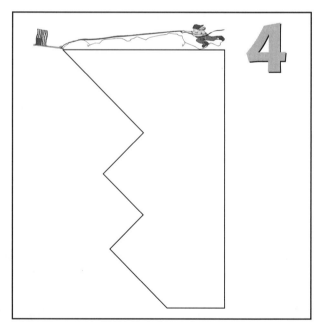

Bonus: Create a new figure using all of the pieces.

Tangram Puzzlers
Geometric Shapes

Blast Off!

1

Math Centers—Take It to Your Seat • EMC 3012

©2002 by Evan-Moor Corp.

2

On the Edge

Tangram

Puzzlers

Geometric Shapes

Tangram

Puzzlers

Geometric Shapes

©2002 by Evan-Moor Corp.

Big Gulp

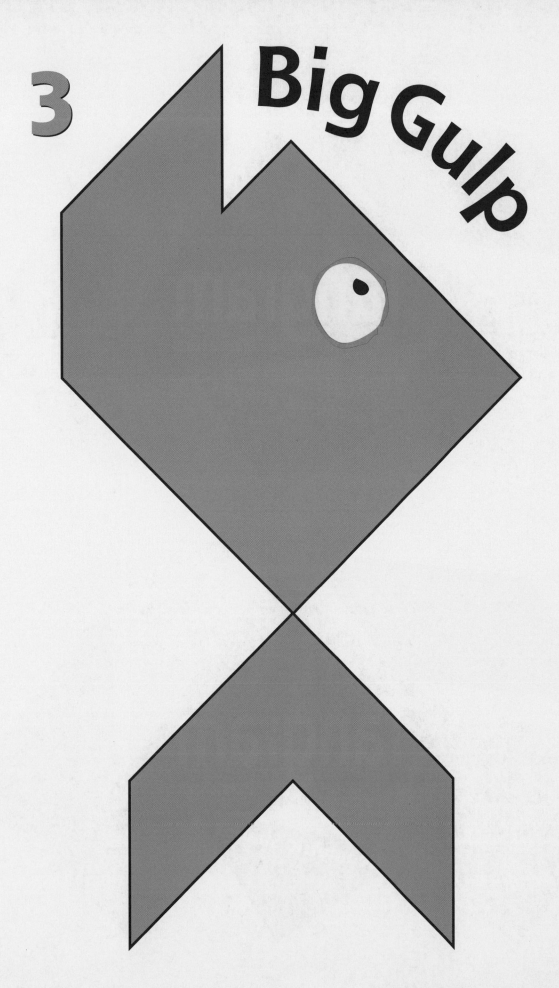

Tangram
Puzzlers

Geometric Shapes

Tangram
Puzzlers

Geometric Shapes

©2002 by Evan-Moor Corp.

Take a Peak!

4

55

Tangram

Puzzlers

Geometric Shapes

Tangram

Puzzlers

Geometric Shapes

©2002 by Evan-Moor Corp.

Take Me Out to the Ballgame

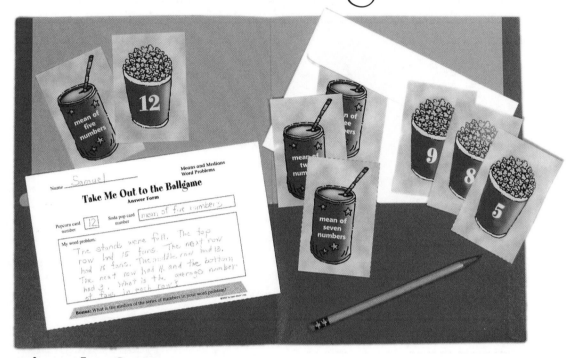

Preparing the Center

1. Prepare a folder following the directions on page 3. Laminate and cut out the cover design on page 59. Attach it to the front of the folder.

2. Laminate and cut out the task cards on pages 61–65. Place them in an envelope and put the envelope in the right-hand pocket of the folder.

3. Reproduce a supply of the answer form on page 58. Place copies in the left-hand pocket of the folder.

Using the Center

1. The student chooses one popcorn task card and one soda pop task card.

2. Then the student creates a word problem that calls for the computation on the soda pop card and is answered by the number on the popcorn card. The student records the problems on the answer form. **Example:**

   soda pop card = average of 5 numbers
   popcorn card = 12
   problem = The stands for spectators at the ballgame
   were full. The top row had 15 fans. The next row had 18 fans. The middle row had 13 fans. The next row had 11 fans, and the bottom row had 3 fans. What is the average number of fans in each row?

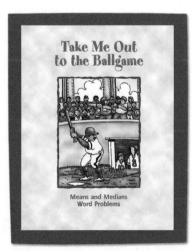

Name _____

Means and Medians
Word Problems

Take Me Out to the Ballgame
Answer Form

Popcorn card
number
[ ]

Soda pop card
number
[   ]

My word problem:

Bonus: What is the median of the series of numbers in your word problem?

©2002 by Evan-Moor Corp.

Name _____

Means and Medians
Word Problems

Take Me Out to the Ballgame
Answer Form

Popcorn card
number
[ ]

Soda pop card
number
[   ]

My word problem:

Bonus: What is the median of the series of numbers in your word problem?

©2002 by Evan-Moor Corp.

Take Me Out to the Ballgame

Means and Medians
Word Problems

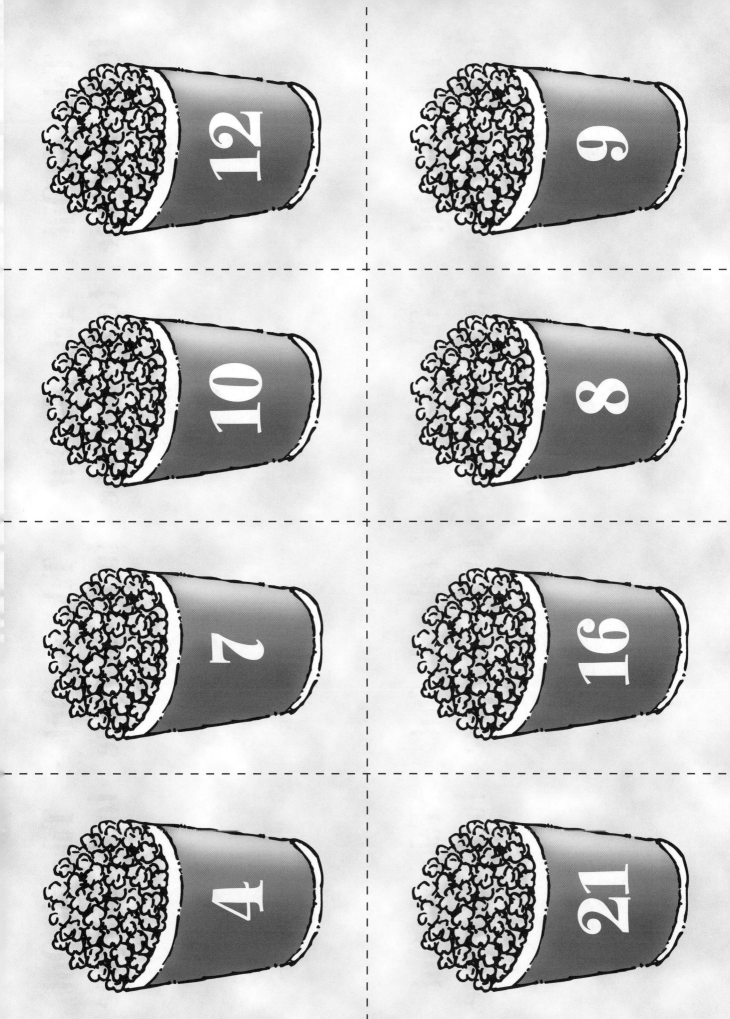

Take Me Out to the Ballgame

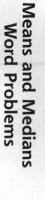

Means and Medians
Word Problems

Take Me Out to the Ballgame

Means and Medians
Word Problems

Take Me Out to the Ballgame

Means and Medians
Word Problems

Take Me Out to the Ballgame

Means and Medians
Word Problems

Take Me Out to the Ballgame

Means and Medians
Word Problems

Take Me Out to the Ballgame

Means and Medians
Word Problems

Take Me Out to the Ballgame

Means and Medians
Word Problems

Take Me Out to the Ballgame

Means and Medians
Word Problems

Take Me Out to the Ballgame

Means and Medians Word Problems

Take Me Out to the Ballgame

Means and Medians Word Problems

Take Me Out to the Ballgame

Means and Medians Word Problems

Take Me Out to the Ballgame

Means and Medians Word Problems

Take Me Out to the Ballgame

Means and Medians Word Problems

Take Me Out to the Ballgame

Means and Medians Word Problems

Take Me Out to the Ballgame

Means and Medians Word Problems

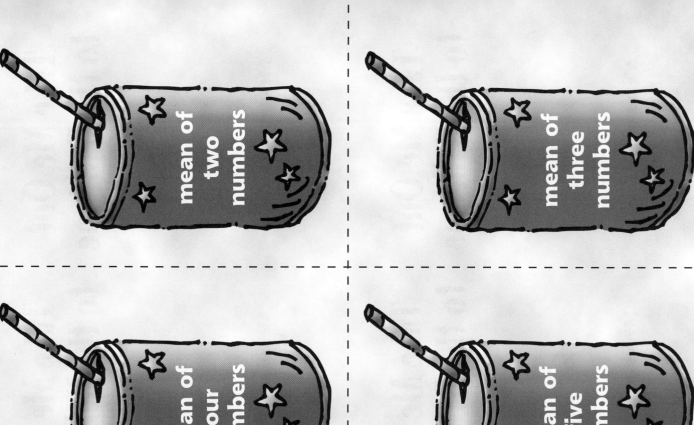

mean of
two
numbers

mean of
three
numbers

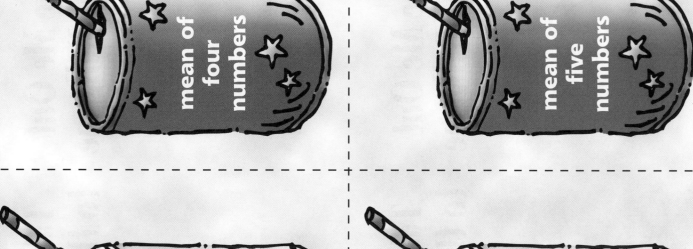

mean of
four
numbers

mean of
five
numbers

mean of
six
numbers

mean of
seven
numbers

mean of
eight
numbers

mean of
nine
numbers

Take Me Out to the Ballgame

**Means and Medians
Word Problems**

©2002 by Evan-Moor Corp.

Take Me Out to the Ballgame

**Means and Medians
Word Problems**

©2002 by Evan-Moor Corp.

Take Me Out to the Ballgame

**Means and Medians
Word Problems**

©2002 by Evan-Moor Corp.

Take Me Out to the Ballgame

**Means and Medians
Word Problems**

©2002 by Evan-Moor Corp.

Take Me Out to the Ballgame

**Means and Medians
Word Problems**

©2002 by Evan-Moor Corp.

Take Me Out to the Ballgame

**Means and Medians
Word Problems**

©2002 by Evan-Moor Corp.

Making Change

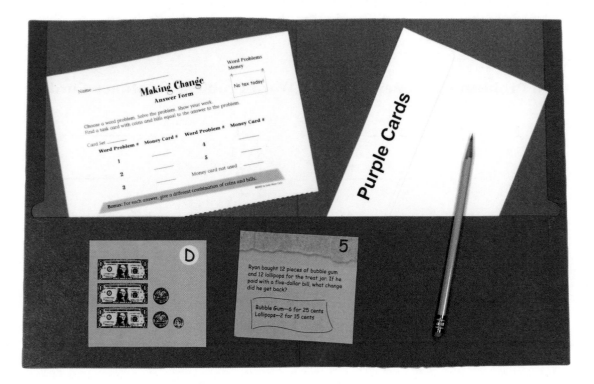

Preparing the Center

1. Prepare a folder following the directions on page 3. Laminate and cut out the cover design on page 69. Attach it to the front of the folder.

2. Laminate and cut out the sets of money task cards and the word problem task cards on pages 71–81. Place them in envelopes, glue the labels to the envelopes, and place the envelopes in the right-hand pocket of the folder.

3. Reproduce a supply of the answer form on page 68. Place copies in the left-hand pocket of the folder.

Using the Center

1. The student chooses a word problem task card.

2. The student solves the problem, and then finds a money task card with coins and bills equal to the answer to the problem.

3. Then the student records the numbers of the two cards on the answer form.

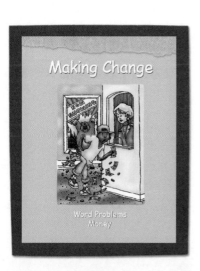

Name _____

Making Change
Answer Form

Word Problems
Money

No tax today!

Choose a word problem. Solve the problem. Show your work.
Find a task card with coins and bills equal to the answer to the problem.

Card Set _____

Word Problem #	Money Card #	Word Problem #	Money Card #
1	_____	4	_____
2	_____	5	_____
3	_____	Money card not used	_____

Bonus: For each answer, give a different combination of coins and bills.

©2002 by Evan-Moor Corp.

Name _____

Making Change
Answer Form

Word Problems
Money

No tax today!

Choose a word problem. Solve the problem. Show your work.
Find a task card with coins and bills equal to the answer to the problem.

Card Set _____

Word Problem #	Money Card #	Word Problem #	Money Card #
1	_____	4	_____
2	_____	5	_____
3	_____	Money card not used	_____

Bonus: For each answer, give a different combination of coins and bills.

©2002 by Evan-Moor Corp.

Making Change

Word Problems
Money

Making Change Set 1

Word Problems—Money

1

Jose and Maria visited the ice-cream store. They each ordered a double-dip rocky road cone. Jose had a sugar cone and Maria had a plain cone. They gave the clerk a ten-dollar bill. What change did they get back?

Single scoop—$1.50

Double scoop—$2.00

Sugar cones 25 cents extra

Penny and Sarah love scrapbooking. They bought 10 pages of colored paper at 4 cents a page, a special pair of shears for $6.99, and some stickers for $4.25. They paid with a twenty-dollar bill. What change did they get back?

Frank bought six sets of trading cards on sale for $1.79 a set. If he paid with three five-dollar bills, what change did he get back?

Vinnie rode the Ferris wheel eight times. Each ride takes one ticket. He bought all of his tickets at the same time so he would get the best price. He paid with a ten-dollar bill. How much change did he get back?

1 ticket—$1.25

4 tickets—$4.00

Tracey went riding. The charge for the horse rental was $12 an hour. Tracey rode for 2 1/2 hours and paid with two twenty-dollar bills. What change did she get back?

Making Change
Set 1
Word Problems—Money
©2002 by Evan-Moor Corp.

Making Change
Set 1
Word Problems—Money
©2002 by Evan-Moor Corp.

Making Change
Set 1
Word Problems—Money
©2002 by Evan-Moor Corp.

Making Change
Set 1
Word Problems—Money
©2002 by Evan-Moor Corp.

Making Change
Set 1
Word Problems—Money
©2002 by Evan-Moor Corp.

Making Change
Set 1
Word Problems—Money
©2002 by Evan-Moor Corp.

Making Change
Set 1
Word Problems—Money

Making Change
Set 1
Word Problems—Money
©2002 by Evan-Moor Corp.

Making Change
Set 1
Word Problems—Money
©2002 by Evan-Moor Corp.

Making Change
Set 1
Word Problems—Money
©2002 by Evan-Moor Corp.

Making Change
Set 1
Word Problems—Money
©2002 by Evan-Moor Corp.

Making Change
Set 1
Word Problems—Money
©2002 by Evan-Moor Corp.

Making Change
Set 2
Word Problems—Money

1

Tickets for the movie cost $4.75 each. If six boys buy their tickets with two twenty-dollar bills, how much change will they get back?

2

Sue bought two tickets for the concert. Each ticket cost $17.50 + $1.50 service fee. She paid for the tickets with two twenty-dollar bills. What change did she get back?

3

Fred and Vicky bought a bouquet of roses for Mrs. Smith. The roses cost $18 a dozen. The bouquet had 18 roses. If they paid for the bouquet with three ten-dollar bills, how much change did they get back?

4

Mrs. Nance bought juice bars for the soccer team. There are twelve girls on the team. If she paid with a ten-dollar bill, how much change did she get back?

YUM Bars
6 in box
$3.29

5

A computer game is on sale for $12.99. If Josh buys the game with the twenty-dollar bill he earned mowing lawns, how much change will he get back?

Making Change
Set 2
Word Problems—Money

Making Change
Set 2
Word Problems—Money

©2002 by Evan-Moor Corp.

Making Change
Set 2
Word Problems—Money

©2002 by Evan-Moor Corp.

Making Change
Set 2
Word Problems—Money

©2002 by Evan-Moor Corp.

Making Change
Set 2
Word Problems—Money

©2002 by Evan-Moor Corp.

Making Change
Set 2
Word Problems—Money

©2002 by Evan-Moor Corp.

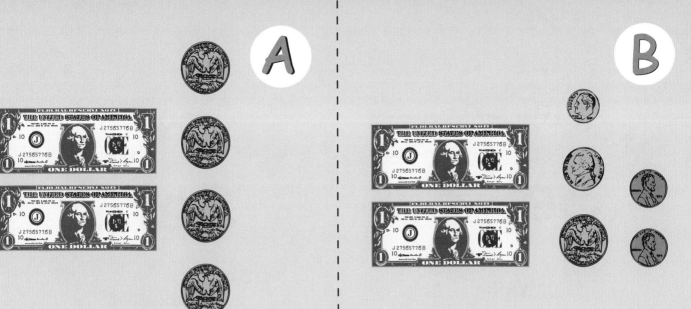

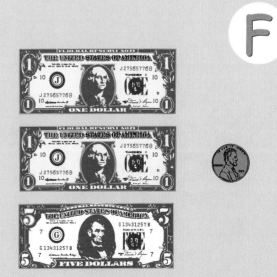

Making Change
Set 2
Word Problems—Money

Making Change
Set 2
Word Problems—Money

Making Change
Set 2
Word Problems—Money

Making Change
Set 2
Word Problems—Money

Making Change
Set 2
Word Problems—Money

Making Change
Set 2
Word Problems—Money

Making Change
Set 3
Word Problems—Money

1

Sonya bought 3 pencils, 6 gel pens, and a black tablet at the store. If she paid with a ten-dollar bill, what change did she get back?

Pencils—3 for $0.50
Gel Pens—2 for $1.00
Black Tablets—$1.75 each

2

Oliver bought two large pizzas for $5.99 each and breadsticks for $3.99. He paid with a twenty-dollar bill. What change did he get back?

3

The cookie shop at the mall has a special—2 cookies for $2.20. After 5 p.m. the cookies are half price. Tom bought ten cookies at 6 p.m. He paid with a ten-dollar bill. What change did he get back?

4

Betty bought special passes to the museum for five friends and herself. Each pass cost $3.50. If she paid with a twenty-dollar bill and a five-dollar bill, what change did she get back?

5

Ryan bought 12 pieces of bubble gum and 12 lollipops for the treat jar. If he paid with a five-dollar bill, what change did he get back?

Bubble Gum—6 for 25 cents
Lollipops—2 for 15 cents

Making Change
Set 3
Word Problems—Money

Making Change
Set 3
Word Problems—Money
©2002 by Evan-Moor Corp.

Making Change
Set 3
Word Problems—Money
©2002 by Evan-Moor Corp.

Making Change
Set 3
Word Problems—Money
©2002 by Evan-Moor Corp.

Making Change
Set 3
Word Problems—Money
©2002 by Evan-Moor Corp.

Making Change
Set 3
Word Problems—Money
©2002 by Evan-Moor Corp.

A

B

C

D

E

F

Making Change
Set 3
Word Problems—Money

Making Change
Set 3
Word Problems—Money

Making Change
Set 3
Word Problems—Money

Making Change
Set 3
Word Problems—Money

Making Change
Set 3
Word Problems—Money

Making Change
Set 3
Word Problems—Money

Be a Builder

Preparing the Center

1. Prepare a folder following the directions on page 3. Laminate and cut out the cover design on page 85. Attach it to the front of the folder.

2. Laminate and cut out the bricks on pages 87 and 89 and the task cards on page 91. Place them in an envelope and put the envelope in the right-hand pocket of the folder.

3. Reproduce a supply of the answer form on page 84. Place copies in the left-hand pocket of the folder.

Using the Center

1. The student selects a task card and builds the room using bricks that equal the perimeter given.

2. Then the student records the perimeter of the room and the dimensions of the room on the record form.

   Note: Corner pieces must be used for each corner of the room.

       Math Centers—Take It to Your Seat • EMC 3012

Name _____

Be a Builder
Answer Form

Choose a task card.
Design a room with the perimeter on the card.
Record the dimensions of the room.

Perimeter chosen: _____

Dimensions of the room:

_____ X _____

Bonus: Calculate the area of the room that you designed.

Name _____

Be a Builder
Answer Form

Choose a task card.
Design a room with the perimeter on the card.
Record the dimensions of the room.

Perimeter chosen: _____

Dimensions of the room:

_____ X _____

Bonus: Calculate the area of the room that you designed.

Name _____

Be a Builder
Answer Form

Choose a task card.
Design a room with the perimeter on the card.
Record the dimensions of the room.

Perimeter chosen: _____

Dimensions of the room:

_____ X _____

Bonus: Calculate the area of the room that you designed.

Name _____

Be a Builder
Answer Form

Choose a task card.
Design a room with the perimeter on the card.
Record the dimensions of the room.

Perimeter chosen: _____

Dimensions of the room:

_____ X _____

Bonus: Calculate the area of the room that you designed.

Be a Builder
Perimeter

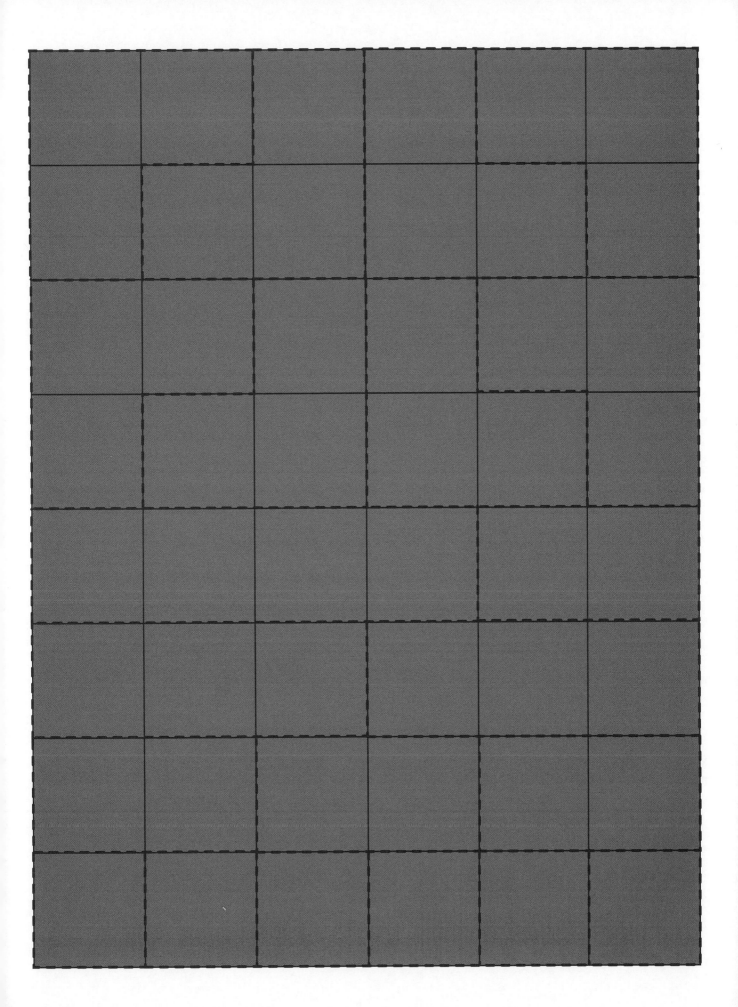

Be a Builder **Perimeter** ©2002 by Evan-Moor Corp.	**Be a Builder** **Perimeter** ©2002 by Evan-Moor Corp.	**Be a Builder** **Perimeter** ©2002 by Evan-Moor Corp.	**Be a Builder** **Perimeter** ©2002 by Evan-Moor Corp.	**Be a Builder** **Perimeter** ©2002 by Evan-Moor Corp.	**Be a Builder** **Perimeter** ©2002 by Evan-Moor Corp.
Be a Builder **Perimeter** ©2002 by Evan-Moor Corp.	**Be a Builder** **Perimeter** ©2002 by Evan-Moor Corp.	**Be a Builder** **Perimeter** ©2002 by Evan-Moor Corp.	**Be a Builder** **Perimeter** ©2002 by Evan-Moor Corp.	**Be a Builder** **Perimeter** ©2002 by Evan-Moor Corp.	**Be a Builder** **Perimeter** ©2002 by Evan-Moor Corp.
Be a Builder **Perimeter** ©2002 by Evan-Moor Corp.	**Be a Builder** **Perimeter** ©2002 by Evan-Moor Corp.	**Be a Builder** **Perimeter** ©2002 by Evan-Moor Corp.	**Be a Builder** **Perimeter** ©2002 by Evan-Moor Corp.	**Be a Builder** **Perimeter** ©2002 by Evan-Moor Corp.	**Be a Builder** **Perimeter** ©2002 by Evan-Moor Corp.
Be a Builder **Perimeter** ©2002 by Evan-Moor Corp.	**Be a Builder** **Perimeter** ©2002 by Evan-Moor Corp.	**Be a Builder** **Perimeter** ©2002 by Evan-Moor Corp.	**Be a Builder** **Perimeter** ©2002 by Evan-Moor Corp.	**Be a Builder** **Perimeter** ©2002 by Evan-Moor Corp.	**Be a Builder** **Perimeter** ©2002 by Evan-Moor Corp.
Be a Builder **Perimeter** ©2002 by Evan-Moor Corp.	**Be a Builder** **Perimeter** ©2002 by Evan-Moor Corp.	**Be a Builder** **Perimeter** ©2002 by Evan-Moor Corp.	**Be a Builder** **Perimeter** ©2002 by Evan-Moor Corp.	**Be a Builder** **Perimeter** ©2002 by Evan-Moor Corp.	**Be a Builder** **Perimeter** ©2002 by Evan-Moor Corp.
Be a Builder **Perimeter** ©2002 by Evan-Moor Corp.	**Be a Builder** **Perimeter** ©2002 by Evan-Moor Corp.	**Be a Builder** **Perimeter** ©2002 by Evan-Moor Corp.	**Be a Builder** **Perimeter** ©2002 by Evan-Moor Corp.	**Be a Builder** **Perimeter** ©2002 by Evan-Moor Corp.	**Be a Builder** **Perimeter** ©2002 by Evan-Moor Corp.
Be a Builder **Perimeter** ©2002 by Evan-Moor Corp.	**Be a Builder** **Perimeter** ©2002 by Evan-Moor Corp.	**Be a Builder** **Perimeter** ©2002 by Evan-Moor Corp.	**Be a Builder** **Perimeter** ©2002 by Evan-Moor Corp.	**Be a Builder** **Perimeter** ©2002 by Evan-Moor Corp.	**Be a Builder** **Perimeter** ©2002 by Evan-Moor Corp.
Be a Builder **Perimeter** ©2002 by Evan-Moor Corp.	**Be a Builder** **Perimeter** ©2002 by Evan-Moor Corp.	**Be a Builder** **Perimeter** ©2002 by Evan-Moor Corp.	**Be a Builder** **Perimeter** ©2002 by Evan-Moor Corp.	**Be a Builder** **Perimeter** ©2002 by Evan-Moor Corp.	**Be a Builder** **Perimeter** ©2002 by Evan-Moor Corp.

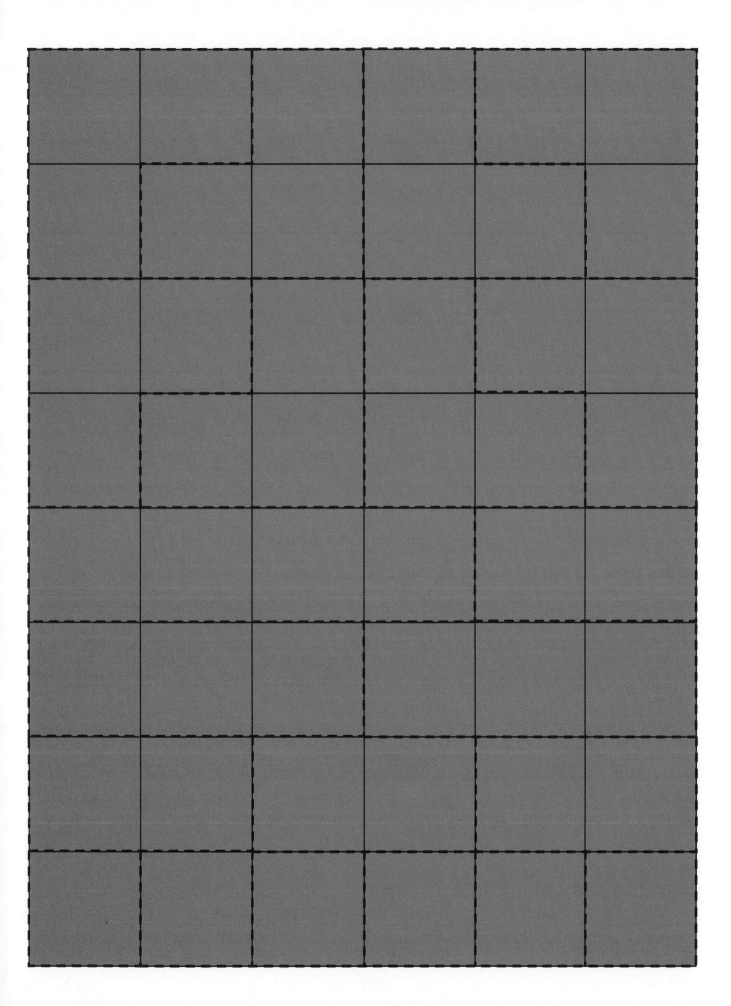

Be a Builder Perimeter ©2002 by Evan-Moor Corp.	Be a Builder Perimeter ©2002 by Evan-Moor Corp.	Be a Builder Perimeter ©2002 by Evan-Moor Corp.	Be a Builder Perimeter ©2002 by Evan-Moor Corp.	Be a Builder Perimeter ©2002 by Evan-Moor Corp.	Be a Builder Perimeter ©2002 by Evan-Moor Corp.
Be a Builder Perimeter ©2002 by Evan-Moor Corp.	Be a Builder Perimeter ©2002 by Evan-Moor Corp.	Be a Builder Perimeter ©2002 by Evan-Moor Corp.	Be a Builder Perimeter ©2002 by Evan-Moor Corp.	Be a Builder Perimeter ©2002 by Evan-Moor Corp.	Be a Builder Perimeter ©2002 by Evan-Moor Corp.
Be a Builder Perimeter ©2002 by Evan-Moor Corp.	Be a Builder Perimeter ©2002 by Evan-Moor Corp.	Be a Builder Perimeter ©2002 by Evan-Moor Corp.	Be a Builder Perimeter ©2002 by Evan-Moor Corp.	Be a Builder Perimeter ©2002 by Evan-Moor Corp.	Be a Builder Perimeter ©2002 by Evan-Moor Corp.
Be a Builder Perimeter ©2002 by Evan-Moor Corp.	Be a Builder Perimeter ©2002 by Evan-Moor Corp.	Be a Builder Perimeter ©2002 by Evan-Moor Corp.	Be a Builder Perimeter ©2002 by Evan-Moor Corp.	Be a Builder Perimeter ©2002 by Evan-Moor Corp.	Be a Builder Perimeter ©2002 by Evan-Moor Corp.
Be a Builder Perimeter ©2002 by Evan-Moor Corp.	Be a Builder Perimeter ©2002 by Evan-Moor Corp.	Be a Builder Perimeter ©2002 by Evan-Moor Corp.	Be a Builder Perimeter ©2002 by Evan-Moor Corp.	Be a Builder Perimeter ©2002 by Evan-Moor Corp.	Be a Builder Perimeter ©2002 by Evan-Moor Corp.
Be a Builder Perimeter ©2002 by Evan-Moor Corp.	Be a Builder Perimeter ©2002 by Evan-Moor Corp.	Be a Builder Perimeter ©2002 by Evan-Moor Corp.	Be a Builder Perimeter ©2002 by Evan-Moor Corp.	Be a Builder Perimeter ©2002 by Evan-Moor Corp.	Be a Builder Perimeter ©2002 by Evan-Moor Corp.
Be a Builder Perimeter ©2002 by Evan-Moor Corp.	Be a Builder Perimeter ©2002 by Evan-Moor Corp.	Be a Builder Perimeter ©2002 by Evan-Moor Corp.	Be a Builder Perimeter ©2002 by Evan-Moor Corp.	Be a Builder Perimeter ©2002 by Evan-Moor Corp.	Be a Builder Perimeter ©2002 by Evan-Moor Corp.
Be a Builder Perimeter ©2002 by Evan-Moor Corp.	Be a Builder Perimeter ©2002 by Evan-Moor Corp.	Be a Builder Perimeter ©2002 by Evan-Moor Corp.	Be a Builder Perimeter ©2002 by Evan-Moor Corp.	Be a Builder Perimeter ©2002 by Evan-Moor Corp.	Be a Builder Perimeter ©2002 by Evan-Moor Corp.

56 Bricks	**34** Bricks	**64** Bricks
58 Bricks	**46** Bricks	**24** Bricks
38 Bricks	**40** Bricks	**66** Bricks
50 Bricks	**68** Bricks	**18** Bricks

Be a Builder
Perimeter Task Cards
©2002 by Evan-Moor Corp.

Be a Builder
Perimeter Task Cards
©2002 by Evan-Moor Corp.

Be a Builder
Perimeter Task Cards
©2002 by Evan-Moor Corp.

Be a Builder
Perimeter Task Cards
©2002 by Evan-Moor Corp.

Be a Builder
Perimeter Task Cards
©2002 by Evan-Moor Corp.

Be a Builder
Perimeter Task Cards
©2002 by Evan-Moor Corp.

Be a Builder
Perimeter Task Cards
©2002 by Evan-Moor Corp.

Be a Builder
Perimeter Task Cards
©2002 by Evan-Moor Corp.

Be a Builder
Perimeter Task Cards
©2002 by Evan-Moor Corp.

Be a Builder
Perimeter Task Cards
©2002 by Evan-Moor Corp.

Be a Builder
Perimeter Task Cards
©2002 by Evan-Moor Corp.

Be a Builder
Perimeter Task Cards
©2002 by Evan-Moor Corp.

Frozen!

Positive and Negative Integers Temperature

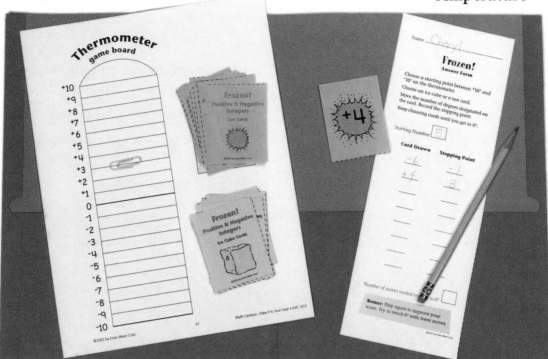

Preparing the Center

1. Prepare a folder following the directions on page 3. Laminate and cut out the cover design on page 95. Attach it to the front of the folder.

2. Laminate page 97. Laminate and cut out the ice cube and sun cards on pages 99 and 101. Place them in an envelope and put the envelope in the right-hand pocket of the folder.

3. Reproduce a supply of the answer form on page 94. Place copies in the left-hand pocket of the folder. Students will need a small piece of paper or a bean to use as a marker.

Using the Center

1. Place the ice cube cards and the sun cards in two piles number side down on the game board.

2. The student chooses a starting number between +10° and −10° on the thermometer and records the number on the answer form and places his marker on the game board. The object of the game is to get to 0° in the fewest number of turns.

3. The student chooses an ice cube card or a sun card from the pile and moves up or down the thermometer the appropriate number of degrees as designated on the card. Each stopping point is then recorded on the record form.

4. The student continues to draw cards and record moves to reach 0°.

Name _____

Frozen!
Answer Form

Choose a starting point between +10° and ⁻10° on the thermometer.

Choose an ice cube or a sun card.

Move the number of degrees designated on the card. Record the stopping point.

Keep choosing cards until you get to 0°.

Starting Number ☐

Card Drawn	Stopping Point
_____	_____
_____	_____
_____	_____
_____	_____
_____	_____
_____	_____
_____	_____
_____	_____

Number of moves needed to reach 0° ☐

Bonus: Play again to improve your score. Try to reach 0° with fewer moves.

Name _____

Frozen!
Answer Form

Choose a starting point between +10° and ⁻10° on the thermometer.

Choose an ice cube or a sun card.

Move the number of degrees designated on the card. Record the stopping point.

Keep choosing cards until you get to 0°.

Starting Number ☐

Card Drawn	Stopping Point
_____	_____
_____	_____
_____	_____
_____	_____
_____	_____
_____	_____
_____	_____
_____	_____

Number of moves needed to reach 0° ☐

Bonus: Play again to improve your score. Try to reach 0° with fewer moves.

Frozen!

Positive & Negative Integers
Temperature

Thermometer
game board

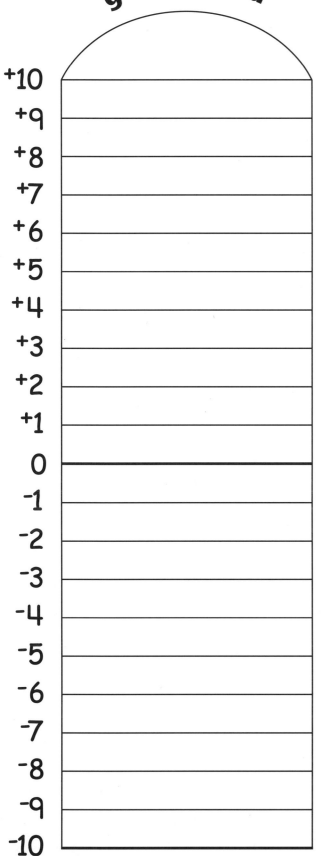

+10
+9
+8
+7
+6
+5
+4
+3
+2
+1
0
-1
-2
-3
-4
-5
-6
-7
-8
-9
-10

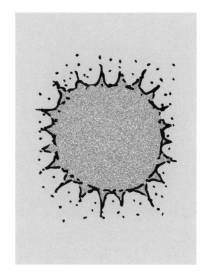

-1	-2	-3	-4
-5	-6	-7	-8
-9	-10	-1	-2
-3	-4	-5	-6

Frozen!
Positive & Negative Integers
Ice Cube Cards

©2002 by Evan-Moor Corp.

Frozen!
Positive & Negative Integers
Ice Cube Cards

©2002 by Evan-Moor Corp.

Frozen!
Positive & Negative Integers
Ice Cube Cards

©2002 by Evan-Moor Corp.

Frozen!
Positive & Negative Integers
Ice Cube Cards

©2002 by Evan-Moor Corp.

Frozen!
Positive & Negative Integers
Ice Cube Cards

©2002 by Evan-Moor Corp.

Frozen!
Positive & Negative Integers
Ice Cube Cards

©2002 by Evan-Moor Corp.

Frozen!
Positive & Negative Integers
Ice Cube Cards

©2002 by Evan-Moor Corp.

Frozen!
Positive & Negative Integers
Ice Cube Cards

©2002 by Evan-Moor Corp.

Frozen!
Positive & Negative Integers
Ice Cube Cards

©2002 by Evan-Moor Corp.

Frozen!
Positive & Negative Integers
Ice Cube Cards

©2002 by Evan-Moor Corp.

Frozen!
Positive & Negative Integers
Ice Cube Cards

©2002 by Evan-Moor Corp.

Frozen!
Positive & Negative Integers
Ice Cube Cards

©2002 by Evan-Moor Corp.

Frozen!
Positive & Negative Integers
Ice Cube Cards

©2002 by Evan-Moor Corp.

Frozen!
Positive & Negative Integers
Ice Cube Cards

©2002 by Evan-Moor Corp.

Frozen!
Positive & Negative Integers
Ice Cube Cards

©2002 by Evan-Moor Corp.

Frozen!
Positive & Negative Integers
Ice Cube Cards

©2002 by Evan-Moor Corp.

Frozen!

Positive & Negative
Integers

Sun Cards

©2002 by Evan-Moor Corp.

Frozen!

Positive & Negative
Integers

Sun Cards

©2002 by Evan-Moor Corp.

Frozen!

Positive & Negative
Integers

Sun Cards

©2002 by Evan-Moor Corp.

Frozen!

Positive & Negative
Integers

Sun Cards

©2002 by Evan-Moor Corp.

Frozen!

Positive & Negative
Integers

Sun Cards

©2002 by Evan-Moor Corp.

Frozen!

Positive & Negative
Integers

Sun Cards

©2002 by Evan-Moor Corp.

Frozen!

Positive & Negative
Integers

Sun Cards

©2002 by Evan-Moor Corp.

Frozen!

Positive & Negative
Integers

Sun Cards

©2002 by Evan-Moor Corp.

Frozen!

Positive & Negative
Integers

Sun Cards

©2002 by Evan-Moor Corp.

Frozen!

Positive & Negative
Integers

Sun Cards

©2002 by Evan-Moor Corp.

Frozen!

Positive & Negative
Integers

Sun Cards

©2002 by Evan-Moor Corp.

Frozen!

Positive & Negative
Integers

Sun Cards

©2002 by Evan-Moor Corp.

Frozen!

Positive & Negative
Integers

Sun Cards

©2002 by Evan-Moor Corp.

Frozen!

Positive & Negative
Integers

Sun Cards

©2002 by Evan-Moor Corp.

Frozen!

Positive & Negative
Integers

Sun Cards

©2002 by Evan-Moor Corp.

Frozen!

Positive & Negative
Integers

Sun Cards

©2002 by Evan-Moor Corp.

Math Messages

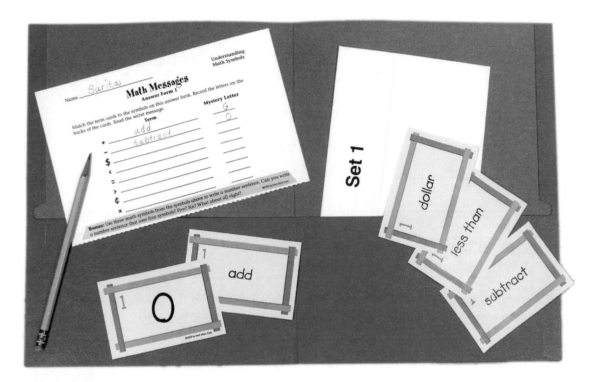

Preparing the Center

1. Prepare a folder following the directions on page 3. Laminate and cut out the cover design on page 105. Attach it to the front of the folder.

2. Laminate and cut out the sets of term cards on pages 107 and 109. Place them in separate envelopes, label the envelopes, and put them in the right-hand pocket of the folder.

3. Reproduce a supply of the answer forms on page 104. Place copies in the left-hand pocket of the folder.

   Note: Answer Form 1 includes the set of symbols to be used with the term cards in Set 1. Answer Form 2 should be used with the term cards in Set 2. Choose the set that is appropriate for your students.

Using the Center

1. The student finds a term card that names each symbol on the answer form.

2. Then the student records the term and the hidden letter on the back of the term card in the appropriate columns on the answer form.

Math Messages
Answer Form 1

Match the term cards to the symbols on this answer form. Record the letters on the backs of the cards. Read the secret message.

	Term	**Mystery Letter**
+	_____	_____
–	_____	_____
$	_____	_____
<	_____	_____
=	_____	_____
>	_____	_____
¢	_____	_____
×	_____	_____

Bonus: Use three math symbols from the symbols above to write a number sentence. Can you write a number sentence that uses four symbols? Five? Six? What about all eight?

©2002 by Evan-Moor Corp.

- -

Math Messages
Answer Form 2

Match the term cards to the symbols on this answer form. Record the letters on the backs of the cards. Read the secret message.

	Term	**Mystery Letter**
≠	_____	_____
∥	_____	_____
π	_____	_____
≅	_____	_____
%	_____	_____
•	_____	_____
÷	_____	_____
≤	_____	_____

Bonus: Use three math symbols from the symbols above to write a number sentence. Can you write a number sentence that uses four symbols? Five? Six? What about all eight?

©2002 by Evan-Moor Corp.

Math Messages

Understanding Math Symbols

1 add	1 subtract
1 dollar	1 less than
1 equal	1 greater than
1 cent	1 multiply

O

1

G

1

D

1

O

1

O

1

W

1

K

1

R

1

2 not equal	2 parallel
2 pi	2 congruent
2 percent	2 decimal point
2 divide	2 less than or equal to

A

M

H

T

H

W

Z

I

Shape Pairs

a game for two players

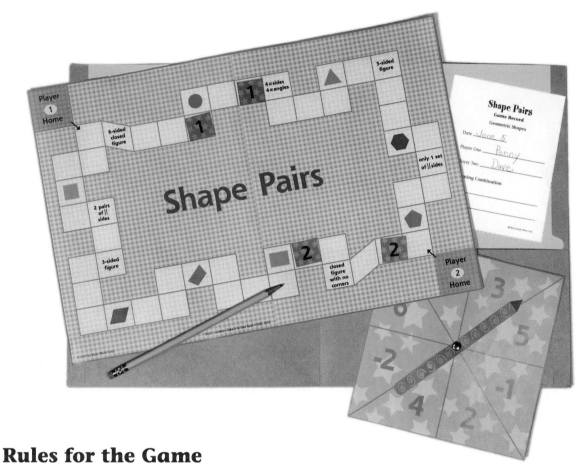

Rules for the Game

The game is over when one player's two playing pieces are on spaces representing the same shape—the picture of a shape and words that accurately describe the shape.

1. Players take turns spinning the spinner and moving one playing piece the number of spaces designated. Positive number moves are made in a clockwise direction. Negative number moves are made in a counterclockwise direction.

2. If Player A lands on a space occupied by Player B, Player B's piece is moved back to the beginning.

3. Play ends when one player's two pieces are on spaces representing the same shape—one figure and one word. **Note:** Several word spaces may describe a single figure. Knowing this becomes part of a player's strategy.

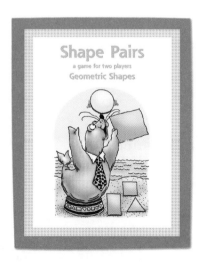

Shape Pairs

Game Record

Geometric Shapes

Date _____

Player One _____

Player Two _____

Winning Combination

Shape _____

Name _____

©2002 by Evan-Moor Corp.

Shape Pairs

Game Record

Geometric Shapes

Date _____

Player One _____

Player Two _____

Winning Combination

Shape _____

Name _____

©2002 by Evan-Moor Corp.

Shape Pairs

Game Record

Geometric Shapes

Date _____

Player One _____

Player Two _____

Winning Combination

Shape _____

Name _____

©2002 by Evan-Moor Corp.

Shape Pairs

Game Record

Geometric Shapes

Date _____

Player One _____

Player Two _____

Winning Combination

Shape _____

Name _____

©2002 by Evan-Moor Corp.

Shape Pairs

a game for two players
Geometric Shapes

Use a paper fastener to attach the arrow to the base of the spinner.

 Math Centers—Take It to Your Seat • EMC 3012

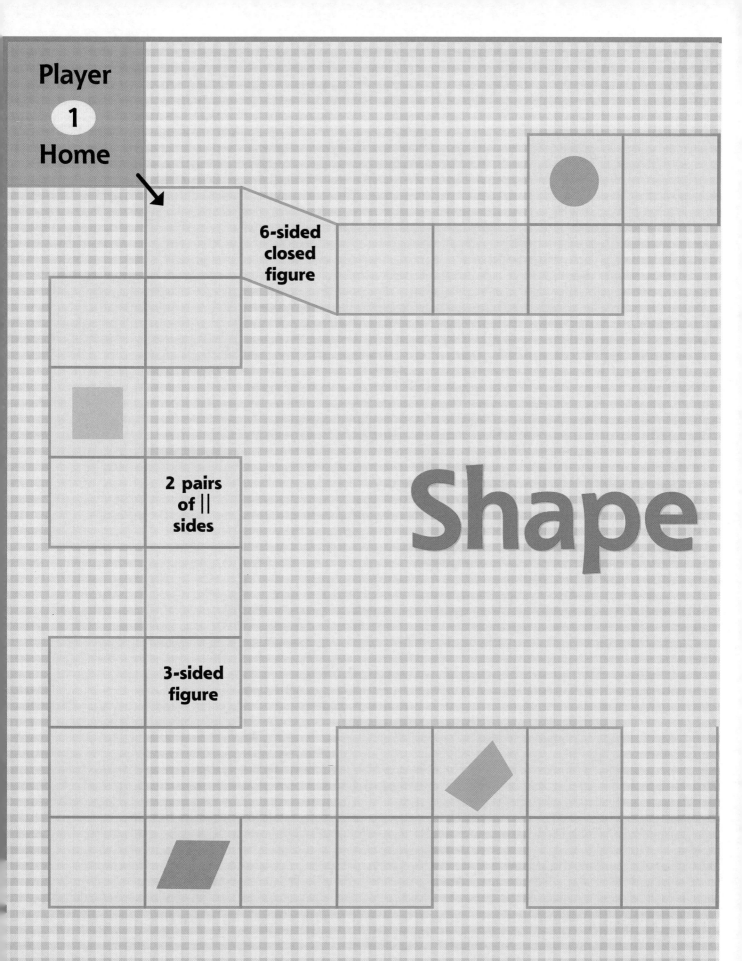

Player

1

Home

6-sided
closed
figure

2 pairs
of || sides

3-sided
figure

Shape

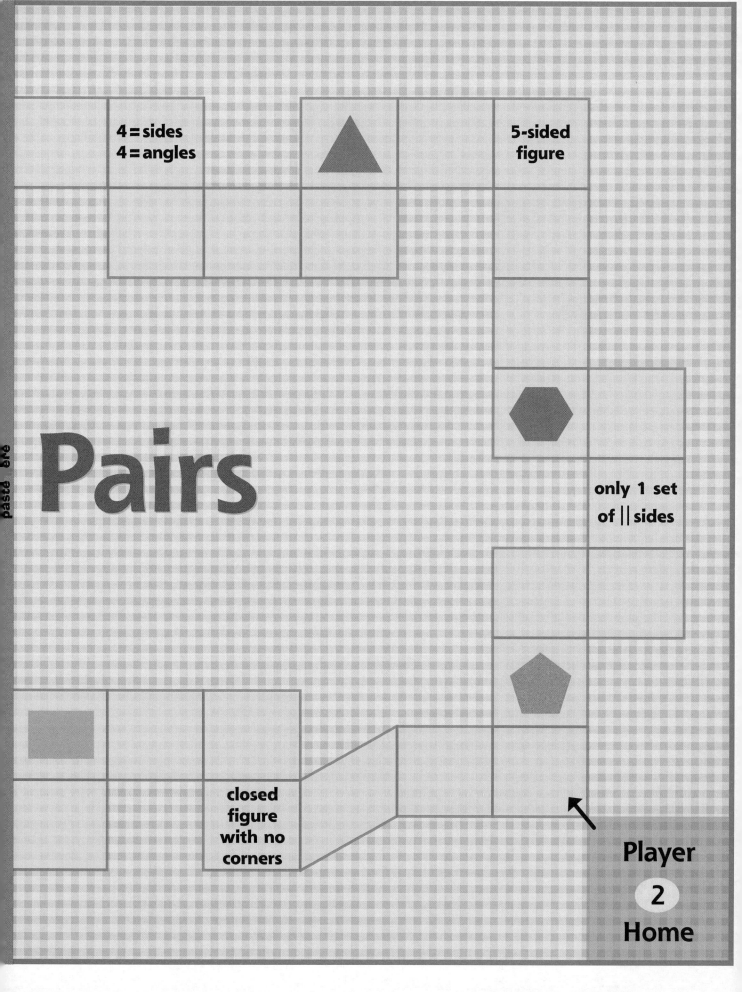

4 = sides
4 = angles

5-sided figure

paste here

Pairs

only 1 set of ‖ sides

closed figure with no corners

Four in a Row
a game for two players

Rules for the Game

The game is over when the four numbers on a player's game board are in consecutive number order.

1. The number cards are stacked in a draw pile, facedown, between the two players. Each player uses one side of the game board.

2. Taking turns, the players draw cards to fill their four spaces on the game board. The first card drawn must be placed in the left-hand space on the board; the next card drawn in the next space, and so on. When each player has filled his or her four number card spaces, turn the top card in the pile over to begin the discard pile.

3. In turn, players may
   - switch the position of two of their cards on the game board, or
   - draw a new card from the draw pile and replace one of their existing number cards, discarding the old card, or
   - take the card on top of the discard pile and replace one of their existing number cards.

4. Play ends when one player's four numbers are in consecutive order from left to right.

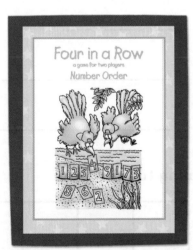

Four in a Row
Game Record
Number Order

Date _____

Time _____

Players _____

_____

Winning Four in a Row

Four in a Row
Game Record
Number Order

Date _____

Time _____

Players _____

_____

Winning Four in a Row

Four in a Row
Games Record
Number Order

Date _____

Time _____

Players _____

_____

Winning Four in a Row

Four in a Row
Game Record
Number Order

Date _____

Time _____

Players _____

_____

Winning Four in a Row

Four in a Row

a game for two players

Number Order

Four in a Row

Number
Card Pile

Math Centers—Take It to Your Seat • EMC 3012

Discard
Pile

Discard
Pile

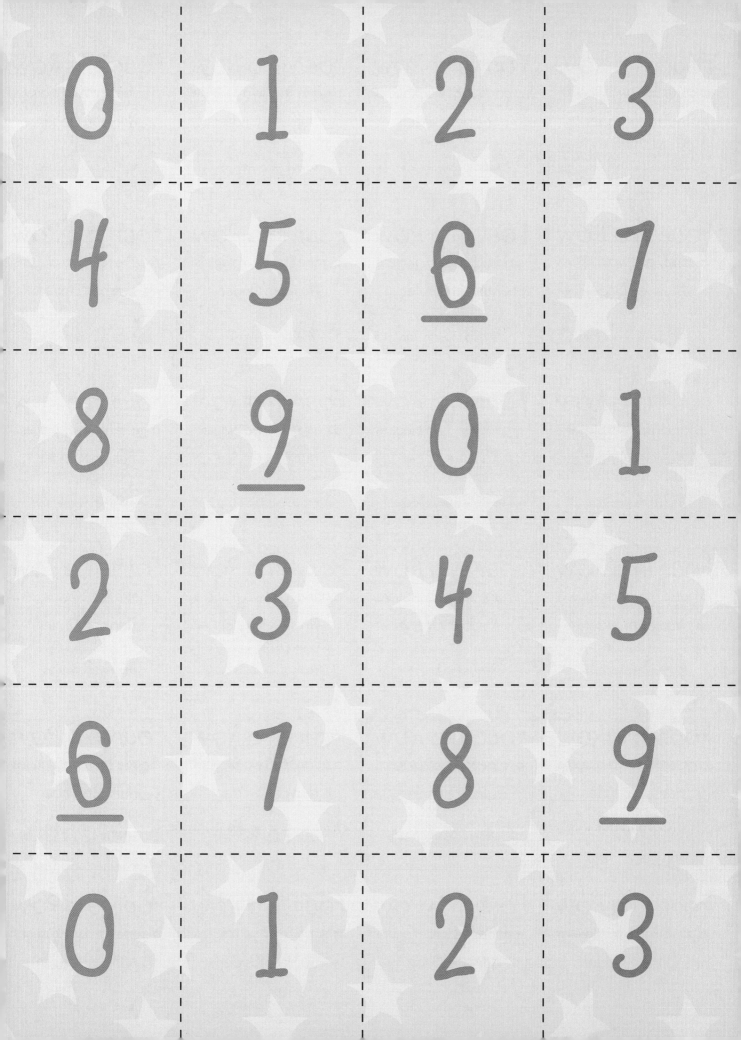

Four in a Row
a game for two players
Number Order

Four in a Row
a game for two players
Number Order

Four in a Row
a game for two players
Number Order

Four in a Row
a game for two players
Number Order

Four in a Row
a game for two players
Number Order

Four in a Row
a game for two players
Number Order

Four in a Row
a game for two players
Number Order

Four in a Row
a game for two players
Number Order

Four in a Row
a game for two players
Number Order

Four in a Row
a game for two players
Number Order

Four in a Row
a game for two players
Number Order

Four in a Row
a game for two players
Number Order

Four in a Row
a game for two players
Number Order

Four in a Row
a game for two players
Number Order

Four in a Row
a game for two players
Number Order

Four in a Row
a game for two players
Number Order

Four in a Row
a game for two players
Number Order

Four in a Row
a game for two players
Number Order

Four in a Row
a game for two players
Number Order

Four in a Row
a game for two players
Number Order

Four in a Row
a game for two players
Number Order

Four in a Row
a game for two players
Number Order

Four in a Row
a game for two players
Number Order

Four in a Row
a game for two players
Number Order

4	5	6	7
8	9	0	1
2	3	4	5
6	7	8	9
0	1	2	3
4	5	6	7

Four in a Row
a game for two players

Number Order

©2002 by Evan-Moor Corp.

Four in a Row
a game for two players

Number Order

©2002 by Evan-Moor Corp.

Four in a Row
a game for two players

Number Order

©2002 by Evan-Moor Corp.

Four in a Row
a game for two players

Number Order

©2002 by Evan-Moor Corp.

Four in a Row
a game for two players

Number Order

©2002 by Evan-Moor Corp.

Four in a Row
a game for two players

Number Order

©2002 by Evan-Moor Corp.

Four in a Row
a game for two players

Number Order

©2002 by Evan-Moor Corp.

Four in a Row
a game for two players

Number Order

©2002 by Evan-Moor Corp.

Four in a Row
a game for two players

Number Order

©2002 by Evan-Moor Corp.

Four in a Row
a game for two players

Number Order

©2002 by Evan-Moor Corp.

Four in a Row
a game for two players

Number Order

©2002 by Evan-Moor Corp.

Four in a Row
a game for two players

Number Order

©2002 by Evan-Moor Corp.

Four in a Row
a game for two players

Number Order

©2002 by Evan-Moor Corp.

Four in a Row
a game for two players

Number Order

©2002 by Evan-Moor Corp.

Four in a Row
a game for two players

Number Order

©2002 by Evan-Moor Corp.

Four in a Row
a game for two players

Number Order

©2002 by Evan-Moor Corp.

Four in a Row
a game for two players

Number Order

©2002 by Evan-Moor Corp.

Four in a Row
a game for two players

Number Order

©2002 by Evan-Moor Corp.

Four in a Row
a game for two players

Number Order

©2002 by Evan-Moor Corp.

Four in a Row
a game for two players

Number Order

©2002 by Evan-Moor Corp.

Four in a Row
a game for two players

Number Order

©2002 by Evan-Moor Corp.

Four in a Row
a game for two players

Number Order

©2002 by Evan-Moor Corp.

Four in a Row
a game for two players

Number Order

©2002 by Evan-Moor Corp.

Four in a Row
a game for two players

Number Order

©2002 by Evan-Moor Corp.

Father Time

a game for two players

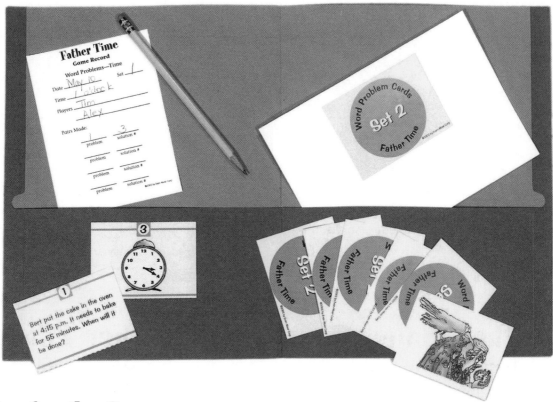

Rules for the Game

The game is over when all the cards have been placed in pairs and one player is left with the Father Time card.

1. The playing cards are shuffled and dealt facedown to the two players.

2. Players lay down any matching pairs they can make using the cards in their hands. A pair consists of a word problem card and a solution card that match.

3. Taking turns, one player draws a card from the other player's hand. Any pairs made are laid down.

4. Play ends when one player holds only the Father Time card.

5. Players record matches on the game record.

Father Time

Game Record

Word Problems—Time

Date _____   Set _____

Time _____

Players _____

_____

Pairs Made:

problem	solution #	problem	solution #
problem	solution #	problem	solution #
problem	solution #	problem	solution #
problem	solution #	problem	solution #

©2002 by Evan-Moor Corp.

Father Time

Game Record

Word Problems—Time

Date _____   Set _____

Time _____

Players _____

_____

Pairs Made:

problem	solution #	problem	solution #
problem	solution #	problem	solution #
problem	solution #	problem	solution #
problem	solution #	problem	solution #

©2002 by Evan-Moor Corp.

Father Time

Game Record

Word Problems—Time

Date _____   Set _____

Time _____

Players _____

_____

Pairs Made:

problem	solution #	problem	solution #
problem	solution #	problem	solution #
problem	solution #	problem	solution #
problem	solution #	problem	solution #

©2002 by Evan-Moor Corp.

Father Time

Game Record

Word Problems—Time

Date _____   Set _____

Time _____

Players _____

_____

Pairs Made:

problem	solution #	problem	solution #
problem	solution #	problem	solution #
problem	solution #	problem	solution #
problem	solution #	problem	solution #

©2002 by Evan-Moor Corp.

Father Time

a game for two players

Word Problems Time

1

It took Kirk 3 hours and 10 minutes to do his homework. If he started at 4 p.m. and took a 30-minute dinner break, when did he finish?

2

Sally practices the piano 2 1/2 hours every evening. If she begins at 6:30 p.m., when will she finish?

3

The trip to Grandma's house will take 6 hours. If Bob's family begins driving at 7:15 a.m. and stops three different times for 20 minutes each time, when will they get there?

4

Lynette pulled weeds for 35 minutes and watered the garden for 20 minutes. If she began at 3:30 p.m., when did she finish?

5

Alex played soccer for 2 hours and 25 minutes. He started at 10 a.m. When did he finish?

6

Mr. Smith ran 6 miles. If it takes him 10 minutes to run a mile and he began running at 5 a.m., when did he finish?

7

Susan walks the dog for 45 minutes. If she starts the walk at 2:20 p.m., when will she be done?

8

Fritz talked on the phone for 14 minutes. If he began talking at 3:50 p.m., when did he finish?

Note: Paste this card on an envelope.

Word Problem Cards

Set 1

Father Time

Word Problem Cards

Set 1

Father Time

Word Problem Cards

Set 1

Father Time

Word Problem Cards

Set 1

Father Time

Word Problem Cards

Set 1

Father Time

Word Problem Cards

Set 1

Father Time

Word Problem Cards

Set 1

Father Time

Word Problem Cards

Set 1

Father Time

Word Problem Cards

Set 1

Father Time

1

Bert put the cake in the oven at 4:15 p.m. It needs to bake for 55 minutes. When will it be done?

2

Cindy Lou walks one block every 2 minutes. If she started walking at 7 a.m. and walked 27 blocks, at what time did she stop?

3

The sewing circle meeting begins at 9:30 a.m. If the meeting lasts for 3 1/2 hours, when will it be over?

4

Farmer Brown milks the cows every morning beginning at 4:30 a.m. He has 20 cows and it takes 10 minutes to milk each cow. When does he finish?

5

The fruit syrup needs to boil for 9 minutes before Aunt Lilly can pour it into the jars. If it started boiling at 1:25 p.m., when can she pour it?

6

Sylvia asked to be excused from school for 2 1/2 hours for an appointment. If she leaves at 11:30 a.m., when will she be back?

7

Kelly's baby brother slept 7 hours last night. If he went to bed at 9 p.m., when did he wake up?

8

Donald completed the puzzle in 50 minutes. If he began at 2:30 p.m., when did he finish?

Note: Paste this card on an envelope.

1

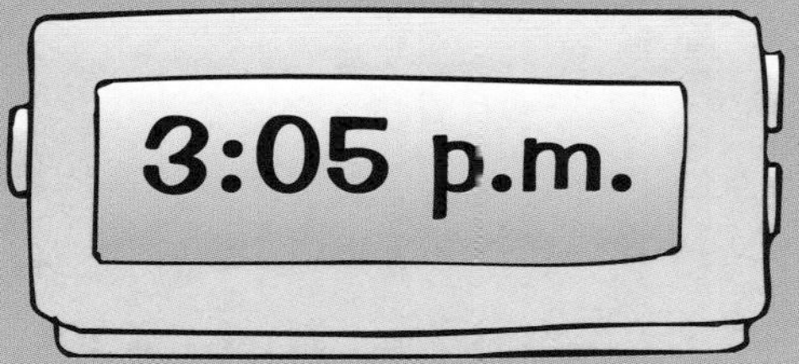
3:05 p.m.

2

12
1
2
3
4
5
6
7
8
9
10
11

3

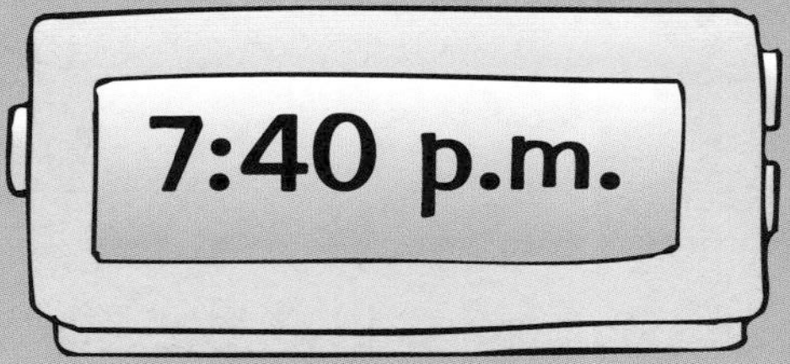
7:40 p.m.

4

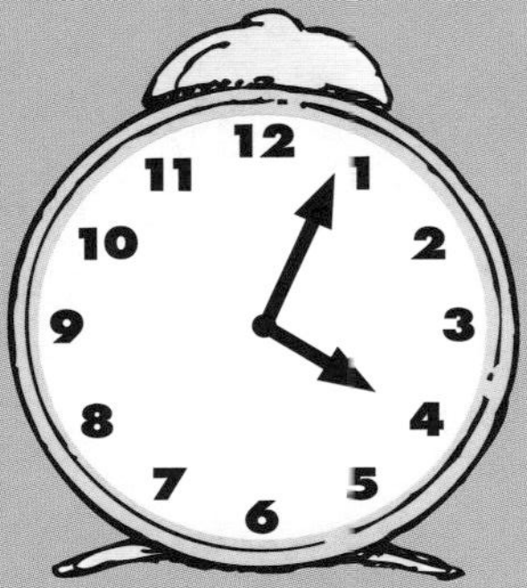
12
1
2
3
4
5
6
7
8
9
10
11

5

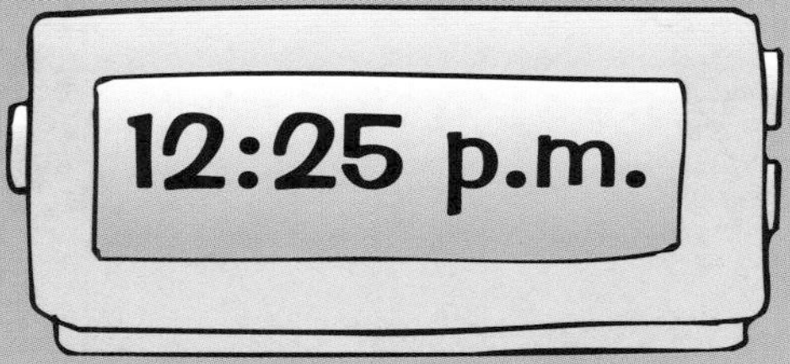
12:25 p.m.

6

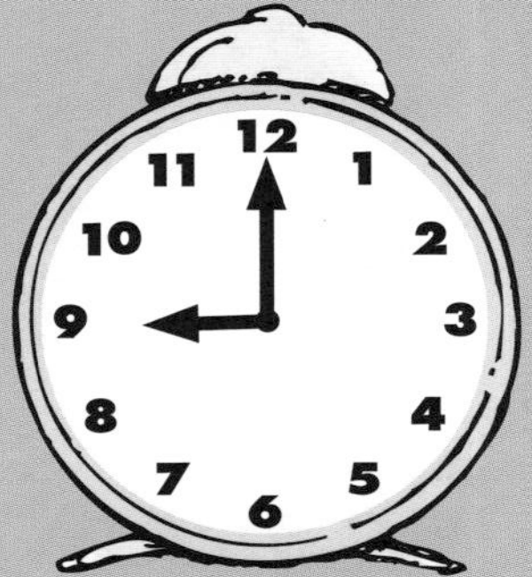
12
1
2
3
4
5
6
7
8
9
10
11

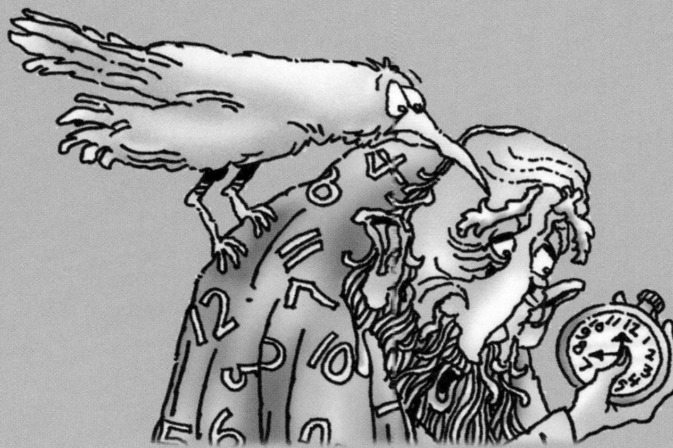

7

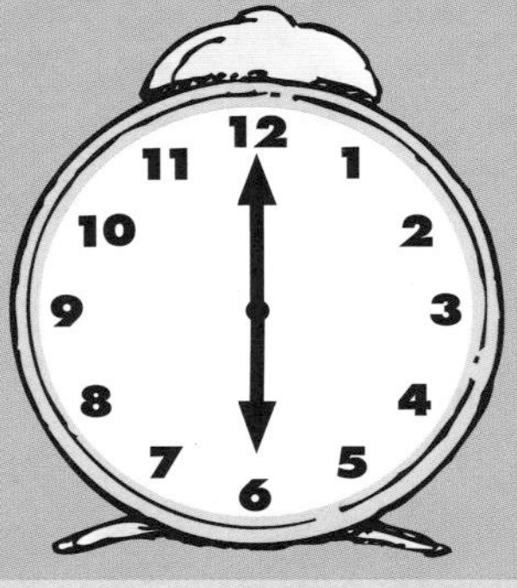
12
1
2
3
4
5
6
7
8
9
10
11

8

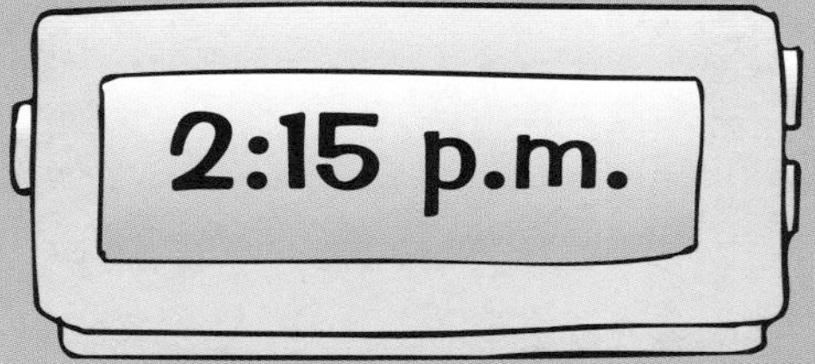
2:15 p.m.

Word Problem Cards

Father Time

Set 1

©2002 by Evan-Moor Corp.

Word Problem Cards

Father Time

Set 1

©2002 by Evan-Moor Corp.

Word Problem Cards

Father Time

Set 1

©2002 by Evan-Moor Corp.

Word Problem Cards

Father Time

Set 1

©2002 by Evan-Moor Corp.

Word Problem Cards

Father Time

Set 1

©2002 by Evan-Moor Corp.

Word Problem Cards

Father Time

Set 1

©2002 by Evan-Moor Corp.

Word Problem Cards

Father Time

Set 1

©2002 by Evan-Moor Corp.

Word Problem Cards

Father Time

Set 1

©2002 by Evan-Moor Corp.

Word Problem Cards

Father Time

Set 1

Word Problem Cards

Set 2

Father Time

Word Problem Cards

Set 2

Father Time

Word Problem Cards

Set 2

Father Time

Word Problem Cards

Set 2

Father Time

Word Problem Cards

Set 2

Father Time

Word Problem Cards

Set 2

Father Time

Word Problem Cards

Set 2

Father Time

Word Problem Cards

Set 2

Father Time

Word Problem Cards

Set 2

Father Time

Factor Fun

a game for two players

Rules for the Game

The game is over when one player reaches 50 points.

1. The green product cards are stacked in a pile, facedown, between the two players. The top card is turned faceup. The purple factor cards are stacked in a pile, facedown, next to the green product cards.

2. Taking turns, the players each draw five purple factor cards.

3. In turn, players use the factor cards in their hands to make an equation that has the product shown on the green product card on top of the pile. The player takes the product card from the pile, lays the cards down, and records the equation on the game record. For each factor card played, 2 points are scored.

4. A new product card is turned over. The player draws cards from the factor pile to replace the cards played. The next player takes a turn.

   Note: If both players are unable to form an equation using the green product card on top of the pile, move the card to the bottom of the pile and try again.

 Math Centers—Take It to Your Seat • EMC 3012

Factor Fun

Game Record

Equations Formed	Points Scored	Total Points
_____	_____	_____
_____	_____	_____
_____	_____	_____
_____	_____	_____
_____	_____	_____
_____	_____	_____
_____	_____	_____

Factor Fun

Game Record

Equations Formed	Points Scored	Total Points
_____	_____	_____
_____	_____	_____
_____	_____	_____
_____	_____	_____
_____	_____	_____
_____	_____	_____

Factor Fun

a game for two players
Multiplication

8	9	10	12
14	15	16	18
20	21	22	24
35	24	27	28

Factor Fun
Product Cards

Multiplication

Factor Fun
Product Cards

Multiplication

Factor Fun
Product Cards

Multiplication

Factor Fun
Product Cards

Multiplication

Factor Fun
Product Cards

Multiplication

Factor Fun
Product Cards

Multiplication

Factor Fun
Product Cards

Multiplication

Factor Fun
Product Cards

Multiplication

Factor Fun
Product Cards

Multiplication

Factor Fun
Product Cards

Multiplication

Factor Fun
Product Cards

Multiplication

Factor Fun
Product Cards

Multiplication

Factor Fun
Product Cards

Multiplication

Factor Fun
Product Cards

Multiplication

Factor Fun
Product Cards

Multiplication

Factor Fun
Product Cards

Multiplication

30	32	32	36
40	42	45	48
49	50	54	56
64	72	81	63

Factor Fun	Factor Fun	Factor Fun	Factor Fun
Product Cards	Product Cards	Product Cards	Product Cards
Multiplication	Multiplication	Multiplication	Multiplication
©2002 by Evan-Moor Corp.	©2002 by Evan-Moor Corp.	©2002 by Evan-Moor Corp.	©2002 by Evan-Moor Corp.
Factor Fun	Factor Fun	Factor Fun	Factor Fun
Product Cards	Product Cards	Product Cards	Product Cards
Multiplication	Multiplication	Multiplication	Multiplication
©2002 by Evan-Moor Corp.	©2002 by Evan-Moor Corp.	©2002 by Evan-Moor Corp.	©2002 by Evan-Moor Corp.
Factor Fun	Factor Fun	Factor Fun	Factor Fun
Product Cards	Product Cards	Product Cards	Product Cards
Multiplication	Multiplication	Multiplication	Multiplication
©2002 by Evan-Moor Corp.	©2002 by Evan-Moor Corp.	©2002 by Evan-Moor Corp.	©2002 by Evan-Moor Corp.
Factor Fun	Factor Fun	Factor Fun	Factor Fun
Product Cards	Product Cards	Product Cards	Product Cards
Multiplication	Multiplication	Multiplication	Multiplication
©2002 by Evan-Moor Corp.	©2002 by Evan-Moor Corp.	©2002 by Evan-Moor Corp.	©2002 by Evan-Moor Corp.

2	2	3	4
5	6	7	8
9	3	4	5
6	7	8	9

Factor Fun
Factor Cards

Multiplication

©2002 by Evan-Moor Corp.

Factor Fun
Factor Cards

Multiplication

©2002 by Evan-Moor Corp.

Factor Fun
Factor Cards

Multiplication

©2002 by Evan-Moor Corp.

Factor Fun
Factor Cards

Multiplication

©2002 by Evan-Moor Corp.

Factor Fun
Factor Cards

Multiplication

©2002 by Evan-Moor Corp.

Factor Fun
Factor Cards

Multiplication

©2002 by Evan-Moor Corp.

Factor Fun
Factor Cards

Multiplication

©2002 by Evan-Moor Corp.

Factor Fun
Factor Cards

Multiplication

©2002 by Evan-Moor Corp.

Factor Fun
Factor Cards

Multiplication

©2002 by Evan-Moor Corp.

Factor Fun
Factor Cards

Multiplication

©2002 by Evan-Moor Corp.

Factor Fun
Factor Cards

Multiplication

©2002 by Evan-Moor Corp.

Factor Fun
Factor Cards

Multiplication

©2002 by Evan-Moor Corp.

Factor Fun
Factor Cards

Multiplication

©2002 by Evan-Moor Corp.

Factor Fun
Factor Cards

Multiplication

©2002 by Evan-Moor Corp.

Factor Fun
Factor Cards

Multiplication

©2002 by Evan-Moor Corp.

Factor Fun
Factor Cards

Multiplication

©2002 by Evan-Moor Corp.

2	3	4	5
6	7	8	9
2	3	4	5
6	7	8	9

Factor Fun Factor Cards Multiplication ©2002 by Evan-Moor Corp.	**Factor Fun** Factor Cards Multiplication ©2002 by Evan-Moor Corp.	**Factor Fun** Factor Cards Multiplication ©2002 by Evan-Moor Corp.	**Factor Fun** Factor Cards Multiplication ©2002 by Evan-Moor Corp.
Factor Fun Factor Cards Multiplication ©2002 by Evan-Moor Corp.	**Factor Fun** Factor Cards Multiplication ©2002 by Evan-Moor Corp.	**Factor Fun** Factor Cards Multiplication ©2002 by Evan-Moor Corp.	**Factor Fun** Factor Cards Multiplication ©2002 by Evan-Moor Corp.
Factor Fun Factor Cards Multiplication ©2002 by Evan-Moor Corp.	**Factor Fun** Factor Cards Multiplication ©2002 by Evan-Moor Corp.	**Factor Fun** Factor Cards Multiplication ©2002 by Evan-Moor Corp.	**Factor Fun** Factor Cards Multiplication ©2002 by Evan-Moor Corp.
Factor Fun Factor Cards Multiplication ©2002 by Evan-Moor Corp.	**Factor Fun** Factor Cards Multiplication ©2002 by Evan-Moor Corp.	**Factor Fun** Factor Cards Multiplication ©2002 by Evan-Moor Corp.	**Factor Fun** Factor Cards Multiplication ©2002 by Evan-Moor Corp.

2	3	4	5
6	7	8	9
2	3	4	5
6	7	8	9

Factor Fun Factor Cards Multiplication ©2002 by Evan-Moor Corp.	**Factor Fun** Factor Cards Multiplication ©2002 by Evan-Moor Corp.	**Factor Fun** Factor Cards Multiplication ©2002 by Evan-Moor Corp.	**Factor Fun** Factor Cards Multiplication ©2002 by Evan-Moor Corp.
Factor Fun Factor Cards Multiplication ©2002 by Evan-Moor Corp.	**Factor Fun** Factor Cards Multiplication ©2002 by Evan-Moor Corp.	**Factor Fun** Factor Cards Multiplication ©2002 by Evan-Moor Corp.	**Factor Fun** Factor Cards Multiplication ©2002 by Evan-Moor Corp.
Factor Fun Factor Cards Multiplication ©2002 by Evan-Moor Corp.	**Factor Fun** Factor Cards Multiplication ©2002 by Evan-Moor Corp.	**Factor Fun** Factor Cards Multiplication ©2002 by Evan-Moor Corp.	**Factor Fun** Factor Cards Multiplication ©2002 by Evan-Moor Corp.
Factor Fun Factor Cards Multiplication ©2002 by Evan-Moor Corp.	**Factor Fun** Factor Cards Multiplication ©2002 by Evan-Moor Corp.	**Factor Fun** Factor Cards Multiplication ©2002 by Evan-Moor Corp.	**Factor Fun** Factor Cards Multiplication ©2002 by Evan-Moor Corp.

That's the Point!

Decimals

a game for two players

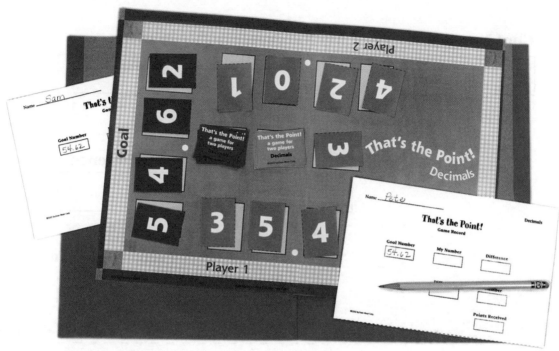

Rules for the Game

At the end of 5 minutes, players calculate the difference between each of their four-digit numbers and the goal number on the game board. The player with the smallest difference is given a point. A point is also given, regardless of the time expired, when a player matches his or her four-digit number to the goal number.

1. The green and red number cards are stacked facedown between the two players on the game board.

2. Taking turns, the players draw red number cards to fill the four spaces of the goal number. Cards may be placed in any open position as they are drawn.

3. In turn, players draw green cards and place them on the game board in their four spaces. Once the spaces have been filled, the player may
   • switch two existing numbers, or
   • draw one card from the draw pile and replace an existing card (The replaced card is discarded.), or
   • take the card on top of the discard pile and replace one of his or her existing number cards.

4. At the end of 5 minutes, players subtract to determine how close they are to the goal number. The closest player is awarded a point.

Name _____

Decimals

That's the Point!

Game Record

Goal Number

My Number

Difference

Opponent's Number

Difference

Points Received

©2002 by Evan-Moor Corp.

- -

Name _____

Decimals

That's the Point!

Game Record

Goal Number

My Number

Difference

Opponent's Number

Difference

Points Received

©2002 by Evan-Moor Corp.

That's the Point!
a game for two players
Decimals

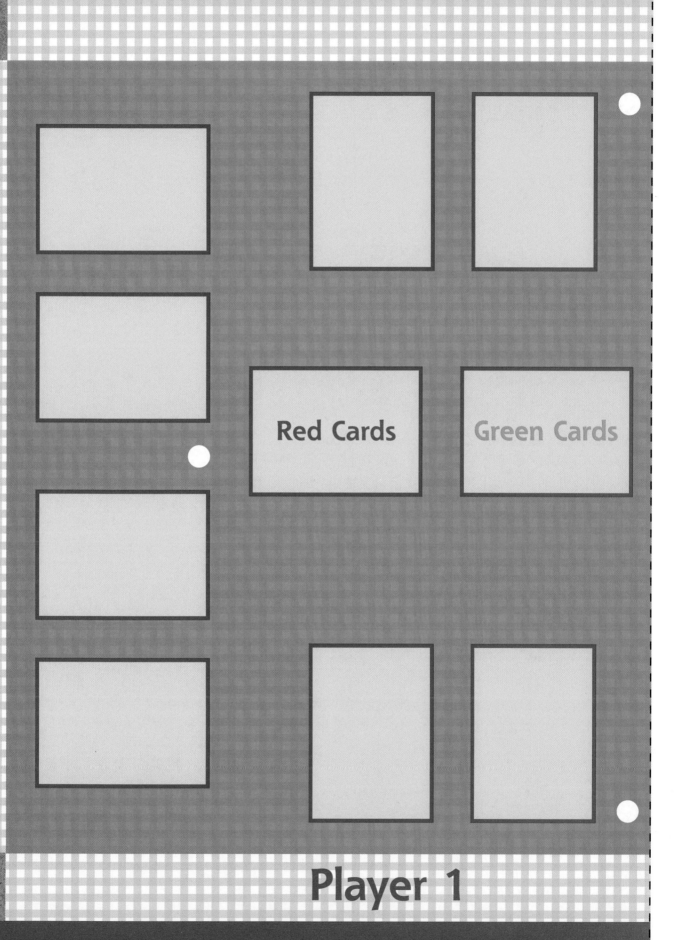

Goal

Red Cards

Green Cards

Player 1

paste here

Discarded

That's the Point!
Decimals

1	2	3
4	5	<u>6</u>
7	8	<u>9</u>

That's the Point!

a game for
two players

Decimals

That's the Point!

a game for
two players

Decimals

©2002 by Evan-Moor Corp.

That's the Point!

a game for
two players

Decimals

©2002 by Evan-Moor Corp.

That's the Point!

a game for
two players

Decimals

©2002 by Evan-Moor Corp.

That's the Point!

a game for
two players

Decimals

©2002 by Evan-Moor Corp.

That's the Point!

a game for
two players

Decimals

©2002 by Evan-Moor Corp.

That's the Point!

a game for
two players

Decimals

©2002 by Evan-Moor Corp.

That's the Point!

a game for
two players

Decimals

©2002 by Evan-Moor Corp.

That's the Point!

a game for
two players

Decimals

©2002 by Evan-Moor Corp.

1	2	3
4	5	<u>6</u>
7	8	<u>9</u>

That's the Point!

a game for two players

Decimals

©2002 by Evan-Moor Corp.

That's the Point!

a game for two players

Decimals

©2002 by Evan-Moor Corp.

That's the Point!

a game for two players

Decimals

©2002 by Evan-Moor Corp.

That's the Point!

a game for two players

Decimals

©2002 by Evan-Moor Corp.

That's the Point!

a game for two players

Decimals

©2002 by Evan-Moor Corp.

That's the Point!

a game for two players

Decimals

©2002 by Evan-Moor Corp.

That's the Point!

a game for two players

Decimals

©2002 by Evan-Moor Corp.

That's the Point!

a game for two players

Decimals

©2002 by Evan-Moor Corp.

That's the Point!

a game for two players

Decimals

©2002 by Evan-Moor Corp.

0	1	2
3	4	5
<u>6</u>	7	8
<u>9</u>	0	1
2	3	4

That's the Point!

a game for
two players

Decimals

©2002 by Evan-Moor Corp.

That's the Point!

a game for
two players

Decimals

©2002 by Evan-Moor Corp.

That's the Point!

a game for
two players

Decimals

©2002 by Evan-Moor Corp.

That's the Point!

a game for
two players

Decimals

©2002 by Evan-Moor Corp.

That's the Point!

a game for
two players

Decimals

©2002 by Evan-Moor Corp.

That's the Point!

a game for
two players

Decimals

©2002 by Evan-Moor Corp.

That's the Point!

a game for
two players

Decimals

©2002 by Evan-Moor Corp.

That's the Point!

a game for
two players

Decimals

©2002 by Evan-Moor Corp.

That's the Point!

a game for
two players

Decimals

©2002 by Evan-Moor Corp.

0	1	2
3	4	5
<u>6</u>	7	8
<u>9</u>	0	1
2	3	4

That's the Point!

a game for
two players

Decimals

©2002 by Evan-Moor Corp.

That's the Point!

a game for
two players

Decimals

©2002 by Evan-Moor Corp.

That's the Point!

a game for
two players

Decimals

©2002 by Evan-Moor Corp.

That's the Point!

a game for
two players

Decimals

©2002 by Evan-Moor Corp.

That's the Point!

a game for
two players

Decimals

©2002 by Evan-Moor Corp.

That's the Point!

a game for
two players

Decimals

©2002 by Evan-Moor Corp.

That's the Point!

a game for
two players

Decimals

©2002 by Evan-Moor Corp.

That's the Point!

a game for
two players

Decimals

©2002 by Evan-Moor Corp.

That's the Point!

a game for
two players

Decimals

©2002 by Evan-Moor Corp.

That's the Point!

a game for
two players

Decimals

©2002 by Evan-Moor Corp.

That's the Point!

a game for
two players

Decimals

©2002 by Evan-Moor Corp.

That's the Point!

a game for
two players

Decimals

©2002 by Evan-Moor Corp.

5	<u>6</u>	7
8	<u>9</u>	0
1	2	3
4	5	<u>6</u>
7	8	<u>9</u>

That's the Point!

a game for
two players

Decimals

©2002 by Evan-Moor Corp.

That's the Point!

a game for
two players

Decimals

©2002 by Evan-Moor Corp.

That's the Point!

a game for
two players

Decimals

©2002 by Evan-Moor Corp.

That's the Point!

a game for
two players

Decimals

©2002 by Evan-Moor Corp.

That's the Point!

a game for
two players

Decimals

©2002 by Evan-Moor Corp.

That's the Point!

a game for
two players

Decimals

©2002 by Evan-Moor Corp.

That's the Point!

a game for
two players

Decimals

©2002 by Evan-Moor Corp.

That's the Point!

a game for
two players

Decimals

©2002 by Evan-Moor Corp.

That's the Point!

a game for
two players

Decimals

©2002 by Evan-Moor Corp.

5	6	7
8	9	0
1	2	3
4	5	6
7	8	9

That's the Point!

a game for two players

Decimals

©2002 by Evan-Moor Corp.

That's the Point!

a game for two players

Decimals

©2002 by Evan-Moor Corp.

That's the Point!

a game for two players

Decimals

©2002 by Evan-Moor Corp.

That's the Point!

a game for two players

Decimals

©2002 by Evan-Moor Corp.

That's the Point!

a game for two players

Decimals

©2002 by Evan-Moor Corp.

That's the Point!

a game for two players

Decimals

©2002 by Evan-Moor Corp.

That's the Point!

a game for two players

Decimals

©2002 by Evan-Moor Corp.

That's the Point!

a game for two players

Decimals

©2002 by Evan-Moor Corp.

That's the Point!

a game for two players

Decimals

©2002 by Evan-Moor Corp.

Try Again!
a game for two players

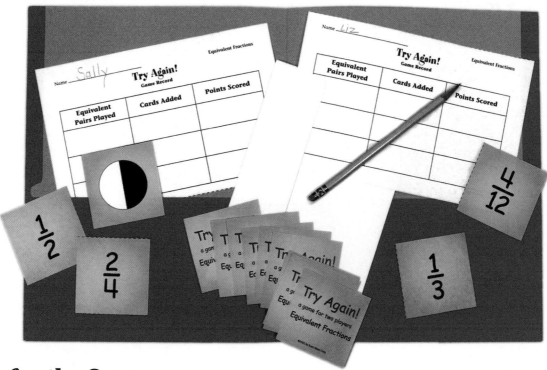

Rules for the Game

The game is over when one player is able to play all the fraction cards in his or her hands.

1. The fraction cards are piled facedown in a draw pile between the two players.

2. Taking turns, the players draw seven fraction cards.

3. Players match equivalent fractions in their hands and place matching sets on the playing surface.

4. Play begins. Player 1 asks Player 2 for a fraction card. "Do you have a fraction card that equals 1/4?" If Player 2 has a matching card, Player 2 gives the card to Player 1. Player 1 lays down any pair created. If Player 2 doesn't have a matching card, Player 2 replies, "Try Again!"

5. Player 1 concludes the turn by drawing a card from the draw pile.

   Note: Once a matching set has been laid down, any player can add another equivalent fraction card to the pair during his or her turn. The point scored for the card goes to the player of the original pair.

Name _____

Try Again!
Game Record

Equivalent Pairs Played	Cards Added	Points Scored

- -

Name _____

Try Again!
Game Record

Equivalent Pairs Played	Cards Added	Points Scored

$$\frac{1}{2}$$

$$\frac{1}{3}$$

$$\frac{1}{4}$$

$$\frac{2}{4}$$

$$\frac{2}{6}$$

$$\frac{2}{8}$$

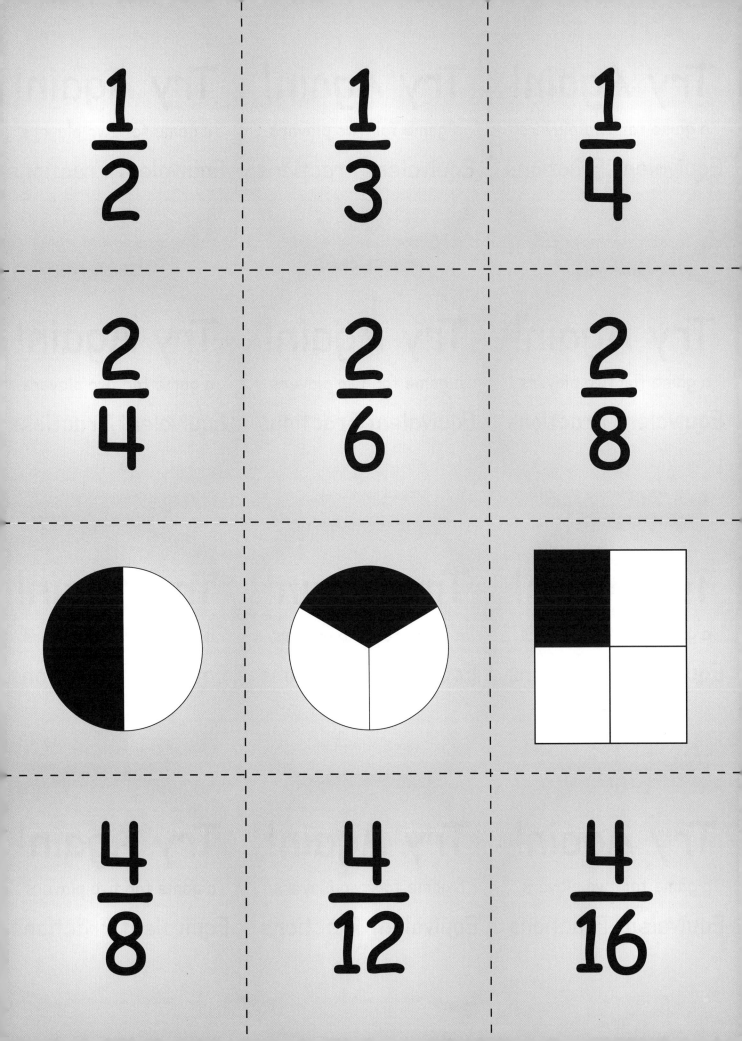

$$\frac{4}{8}$$

$$\frac{4}{12}$$

$$\frac{4}{16}$$

Try Again!

a game for two players

Equivalent Fractions

Try Again!

a game for two players

Equivalent Fractions

Try Again!

a game for two players

Equivalent Fractions

Try Again!

a game for two players

Equivalent Fractions

Try Again!

a game for two players

Equivalent Fractions

Try Again!

a game for two players

Equivalent Fractions

Try Again!

a game for two players

Equivalent Fractions

Try Again!

a game for two players

Equivalent Fractions

Try Again!

a game for two players

Equivalent Fractions

Try Again!

a game for two players

Equivalent Fractions

Try Again!

a game for two players

Equivalent Fractions

Try Again!

a game for two players

Equivalent Fractions

$$\frac{1}{5}$$

$$\frac{1}{6}$$

$$\frac{1}{8}$$

$$\frac{2}{10}$$

$$\frac{2}{12}$$

$$\frac{2}{16}$$

$$\frac{4}{20}$$

$$\frac{4}{24}$$

$$\frac{4}{32}$$

Try Again!

a game for two players

Equivalent Fractions

Try Again!

a game for two players

Equivalent Fractions

Try Again!

a game for two players

Equivalent Fractions

Try Again!

a game for two players

Equivalent Fractions

Try Again!

a game for two players

Equivalent Fractions

Try Again!

a game for two players

Equivalent Fractions

Try Again!

a game for two players

Equivalent Fractions

Try Again!

a game for two players

Equivalent Fractions

Try Again!

a game for two players

Equivalent Fractions

Try Again!

a game for two players

Equivalent Fractions

Try Again!

a game for two players

Equivalent Fractions

Try Again!

a game for two players

Equivalent Fractions

$$\frac{2}{3}$$

$$\frac{3}{4}$$

$$\frac{3}{8}$$

$$\frac{4}{6}$$

$$\frac{6}{8}$$

$$\frac{6}{16}$$

$$\frac{8}{12}$$

$$\frac{9}{12}$$

$$\frac{9}{24}$$

Try Again!

a game for two players

Equivalent Fractions

Try Again!

a game for two players

Equivalent Fractions

Try Again!

a game for two players

Equivalent Fractions

Try Again!

a game for two players

Equivalent Fractions

Try Again!

a game for two players

Equivalent Fractions

Try Again!

a game for two players

Equivalent Fractions

Try Again!

a game for two players

Equivalent Fractions

Try Again!

a game for two players

Equivalent Fractions

Try Again!

a game for two players

Equivalent Fractions

Try Again!

a game for two players

Equivalent Fractions

Try Again!

a game for two players

Equivalent Fractions

Try Again!

a game for two players

Equivalent Fractions

$$\frac{3}{5} \qquad \frac{5}{6} \qquad \frac{7}{8}$$

$$\frac{6}{10} \qquad \frac{10}{12} \qquad \frac{14}{16}$$

$$\frac{9}{15} \qquad \frac{15}{18} \qquad \frac{21}{24}$$

Try Again!

a game for two players

Equivalent Fractions

Try Again!

a game for two players

Equivalent Fractions

Try Again!

a game for two players

Equivalent Fractions

Try Again!

a game for two players

Equivalent Fractions

Try Again!

a game for two players

Equivalent Fractions

Try Again!

a game for two players

Equivalent Fractions

Try Again!

a game for two players

Equivalent Fractions

Try Again!

a game for two players

Equivalent Fractions

Try Again!

a game for two players

Equivalent Fractions

Answer Key

On Sale–page 4

Set 1–Pants
1. $7
2. $5
3. $9
4. $15

Set 1–Shirts
1. $4
2. $12
3. $9
4. $7.50

Set 2—Pants
1. $15
2. $20
3. $8.50
4. $21

Set 2—Shirts
1. $7.50
2. $15
3. $10.50
4. $4

Set 3—Pants
1. $20.40
2. $18.90
3. $16.20
4. $18

Set 3—Shirts
1. $9.50
2. $20.80
3. $12.60
4. $11.90

Comparisons will depend on which cards were selected by the students.

In Balance–page 21

Red Cards
1 pound = 16 ounces
2 pounds = 32 ounces

1 ton = 2000 pounds
2 tons = 4000 pounds
3 tons = 6000 pounds

Blue Cards
1 1/2 pounds = 24 ounces
100 pounds = 1600 ounces
10 pounds = 160 ounces
25 pounds = 400 ounces
50 pounds = 800 ounces

Green Cards
1 kg = 1000 g
1 g = 1/1000 kg
50 g = 1/20 kg
10 g = 1/100 kg
100 g = 1/10 kg

What's Your Angle?– page 31

Answer Form 1, Task Card 1
Angles—3
Sides—3
Name of shape—right triangle

Answer Form 2, Task Card 1
Sum of angles—180°

Answer Form 1, Task Card 2
Angles—3
Sides—3
Name of shape—triangle

Answer Form 2, Task Card 2
Sum of angles—180°

Answer Form 1, Task Card 3
Angles—4
Sides—4
Name of shape—trapezoid

Answer Form 2, Task Card 3
Sum of angles—360°

Answer Form 1, Task Card 4
Angles—4
Sides—4
Name of shape—square

Answer Form 2, Task Card 4
Sum of angles—360°

Answer Form 1, Task Card 5
Angles—4
Sides—4
Name of shape—trapezoid

Answer Form 2, Task Card 5
Sum of angles—360°

Answer Form 1, Task Card 6
Angles—4
Sides—4
Name of shape—square

Answer Form 2, Task Card 6
Sum of angles—360°

Answer Form 1, Task Card 7
Angles—3
Sides—3
Name of shape—triangle

Answer Form 2, Task Card 7
Sum of angles—180°

Answer Form 1, Task Card 8
Angles—3
Sides—3
Name of shape—triangle

Answer Form 2, Task Card 8
Sum of angles 180°

Answer Form 1, Task Card 9
Angles—4
Sides—4
Name of shape—rectangle

Answer Form 2, Task Card 9
Sum of angles—360°

Answer Form 1, Task Card 10
Angles—5
Sides—5
Name of shape—pentagon

Answer Form 2, Task Card 10
Sum of angles—540°

Answer Form 1, Task Card 11
Angles—5
Sides—5
Name of shape—pentagon

Answer Form 2, Task Card 11
Sum of angles—540°

Answer Form 1, Task Card 12
Angles—3
Sides—3
Name of shape—right triangle

Answer Form 2, Task Card 12
Sum of angles—180°

Answer Form 1, Task Card 13
Angles—8
Sides—8
Name of shape—octagon

Answer Form 2, Task Card 13
Sum of angles—1080°

Answer Form 1, Task Card 14
Angles—3
Sides—3
Name of shape—triangle

Answer Form 2, Task Card 14
Sum of angles—180°

Answer Form 1, Task Card 15
Angles—4
Sides—4
Name of shape—parallelogram

Answer Form 2, Task Card 15
Sum of angles—360°

Answer Form 1, Task Card 16
Angles—3
Sides—3
Name of shape—triangle

Answer Form 2, Task Card 16
Sum of angles—180°

Answer Form 1, Task Card 17
Angles—4
Sides—4
Name of shape—parallelogram

Answer Form 2, Task Card 17
Sum of angles—360°

Answer Form 1, Task Card 18
Angles—3
Sides—3
Name of shape—triangle

Answer Form 2, Task Card 18
Sum of angles—180°

Tangram Puzlers– page 43

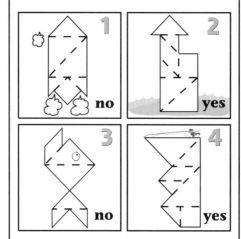

Take Me Out to the Ballgame–page 57

Answers will vary with student's selection of cards.

Making Change– page 67

Set 1—Word Problems
1. $5.75   matches money card F
2. $8.36   matches money card C
3. $4.26   matches money card E
4. $2.00   matches money card D
5. $10.00 matches money card A

Set 2—Word Problems
1. $11.50 matches money card D
2. $2.00   matches money card E
3. $3.00   matches money card A
4. $3.42   matches money card C
5. $7.01   matches money card F

Set 3—Word Problems
1. $4.75   matches money card A
2. $4.03   matches money card B
3. $4.50   matches money card F
4. $4.00   matches money card C
5. $3.60   matches money card D

Be a Builder–page 83

Dimensions of the rooms will vary, but must result in the perimeter drawn.

Frozen!–page 93

The number of cards used will vary depending on the starting temperature chosen and the ice and/or sun cards drawn.

Math Messages– page 103

Set 1—Good Work
Set 2—Math Whiz

Shape Pairs–page 111

Possible winning combinations:

6-sided closed figure = (hexagon)

closed figure with no corners = (circle)

4 = sides and 4 = angles = (square)

2 pairs of || sides = (square) **or** (parallelogram) **or** (rectangle)